Russian Design
1920 – 1990

Alexander N. Lavrentiev
Yuri V. Nasarov

Russian Design
Tradition and Experiment
1920 – 1990

A.R. ACADEMY EDITIONS

Frontispiece   Sachar Bykov: convertible lamp with circular panel and triangular form, 1922, constructed in 1979 by Alexander Lavrentievre.

Original edition
© 1995 Ernst & Sohn, Verlag für Architektur und technische Wissenschaften GmbH, Berlin
English edition first published in Great Britain by
ACADEMY EDITIONS

An imprint of
ACADEMY GROUP
42 Leinster Gardens, London W2 3AN

Ernst & Sohn and Academy Group are members of the VCH Publishing Group.

Distributed to the trade in the United States of America by
ST MARTIN'S PRESS, 175 Fifth Avenue, New York, NY 10012

ISBN 1 85490 426 4

Design: Alexander N. Lavrentiev
Cover Design: Andrea Bettella and Sonia Brooks-Fisher

Translation from German: Flora Fischer
Editorial: Ramona Khambatta

Typesetting: SiB · Satzzentrum in Berlin GmbH, Berlin
Reproduction: Reprowerkstatt Rink, Berlin
Printing: Ratzlow-Druck, Berlin
Binding: B. Helm, Berlin

Production: Fred Willer, Berlin

Contents

2 Entrance to the Soviet Section of the 'Exposition Internationale des Arts Décoratifs et Industriels modernes' in Paris, Grand Palais, 1925. Photo: Henri Manuel.

3 Vladimir Tatlin: Design for the *Monument for the III International,* 1919–20.

INTRODUCTION

In Russia it is often believed that design is more of an intellectual creation on the part of designers, rather than concepts which are realised in practical form. Everyday objects and similar items appear to be conjured up more as creations of the imagination, according to some idea of perfection, than as concrete forms of industrial products.

Such preconceptions cannot be entirely dismissed. One of the aims of this book is to give an idea of the two sides of Russian design: the creative passion of designers, their ideas and the search for an adequate form; and the actual circumstances of the everyday working world, which is often only ready to accept changes after great resistance. At the same time, it is a fact that the intellectual, artistic and technical élites were involved in design in the last seventy years. They were neither laymen, dreamers, nor out of touch with reality.

There are exceptions whereby highly aesthetic designs with revolutionary technical solutions were used as models for mass-produced items only after countless changes – if at all. Apart from the Moscow Underground, work from advertising and book design (mainly posters) and models for lamps from the twenties, could be cited as examples. On the whole it already meant a great deal if interesting designs were shown to the public – as unique examples, patterns or models. This influenced production indirectly. It could, for example,

provide impulses for considering possibilities for modernisation. Reasons for the hesitant approach by industry were a result of the fixation with the attempt to keep pace with the developments in other countries, or even to overtake them, as well as contending with the backwardness of the market and the takeover of old technology and production facilities from Europe and America.

The development of design into an autonomous art form is closely linked to the October Revolution of 1917 and its influence on all aspects of political, social and cultural life. The new release of inventiveness and creativity called upon artists to identify with the mass of workers and farmers and to ameliorate their often depressing lifestyles with courageous projects, to design great public demonstrations and to plan cities of the future. The design forms of those years were those of the artistic avant-garde, in so far as art and design, and design and pictorial experiment were not interchangeable. A precise division of the two hardly appears possible even today.

Although production distanced itself from the designs offered by progressive designers, it was also the case that design acted as a stimulant for industry to a certain extent. The artist was hence not simply a creator but also an advertiser for his work. At the same time, he could, or had to, take on a role in production that was unfamiliar, becoming a technically adept expert or designer who was responsible for the creation of optimal working conditions in factories.

4 Display window of the Design Centre in Moscow, 1980s.

The industrial standardisation that took place in the thirties was developed from similar ideas in the avant-garde design of so-called *production art.* There were also impulses and influences from abroad. These were seized upon all the more readily if serial and mass production promised quicker availability of consumer goods for the population. Standardisation was therefore a recipe against lack of availability, low quality and dissatisfaction. It could not provide solutions for everything, although in the long run it was a successful aspect of the slow process of industrialisation, demanding innovation and providing work for a large number of designers.

The respect paid to designers in contemporary Russia is the same as that paid to artists. As has been the case in other countries, this prestige has gradually been consolidated by developing new, highly original projects. At the same time, it must be remembered that the high level of Russian design (which has also been acknowledged internationally) could not have been reached without the experiments made in photography, painting, sculpture and decorative arts in the past two decades. These experiments often consciously developed ideas from the twenties and early thirties within the framework of a general historical perspective and research into the past. This artistic legacy, hidden in archives and depots that were closed to the public for decades, is now being reassessed academically. As regards Russian design, it can be seen that in times of change theories often race ahead of practice. This is a phenomenon typical of the present situation.

Industrial design had to be in accordance with State interests and Party demands until long after the Stalin era. This created numerous problems, not solely in the area of good taste and aesthetics. The groups displaying an often remarkable incompetence in matters of style – not designers themselves – decided what was progressive and modern or simply what was practical and functional. For example, there were many debates simply about the acceptability of streamlined forms in the thirties.

Design increasingly became a tool used for ideological indoctrination. As was the case with the visual and performing arts, design was used to teach class consciousness, help mitigate 'damaging' and 'formalistic' foreign influences and demonstrate the superiority of the Socialist system over others. It therefore mirrored Soviet social structures in a rather conventional manner until the late forties, appearing to return to pre-revolutionary ideas of beauty and rejecting the experiments of the twenties. As the State controlled their work, designers were forced to suspend foreign contacts.

A new course could only be taken towards the end of the Stalin era. There was a change in official cultural politics, although this by no means meant a fundamental relinquishing of the often grotesque means and methods whereby State and Party structured the arts. Ministerial bodies still decided on matters of style although controls could no longer hinder the emergence of certain liberal tendencies. This was expressed in a reappraisal of the art

5 Moscow Design Exhibition, 1982. Photo: V Kosiakin.

of the twenties, for example. There were clear attempts to comply with, or at least orientate oneself with, international standards in the form of industrial products – including furniture, clothes and consumer goods.

At the same time, the system of State design offices was consolidated. For the first time in history, the professional image of the designer received clearer contours. The specific characteristics of his activities emerged clearly, so that they could be distinguished from those of engineering, model building or technical drawing. This, however, changed little in the bureaucratisation of design, under the aegis of a Socialist planned economy with all its limitations. Federal norms for colours and material, for the quality of products and the ways in which they could be used, hardly allowed for great freedom.

A true renewal of the democratic traditions of design was only possible after the collapse of the old political system (although the experiments in *paper design* in the sixties and seventies were noteworthy). Design appeared to distance itself from politics (or vice versa). It changed its forms and became commercial. In several areas, such as advertising, packaging, and book and newpaper design, it attempted to cater to higher levels and greater demand, thereby losing ground in the area of product design.

As regards form, design has allied itself to international trends. Any survey such as that attempted by this book must, however, take into account the symptoms of crises that darken the picture of Russian design, despite all the signs pointing towards a fruitful renewal. These symptoms are of a primarily economic nature and should be studied with understanding, patience and a view to help, both at home and abroad.

THE REVOLUTION OF FORM

1

7

8

6 Alexander Rodchenko: Design
for an Airport, 1919.

7 Demonstration and parade on
the occasion of the 3rd Anniversary of the October Revolution on
Red Square, Mosow, November
1920. – 8 Gustav Klutsis: design
for the *Radio-orator No. 5,* an
agitatory machine, 1922.

The Revolution of Form

We were the inventors and formed the world
in our own manner.
Alexander M Rodchenko

The basis of what is now called industrial
form or, more generally, design, came into
being in nineteenth-century Russia. The long
duration of the School for Design in Art and
Crafts – re-named the First Free State Art Studios in 1918, and had been initiated by Count
Stroganov in Moscow in 1825 – was particularly inspirational and encouraging for the
manufacture of everyday objects whose outward appearance was influenced by aesthetic,
as well as functional, considerations. Towards
the end of the century, similar schools and
institutes could be found in St Petersburg,
as well as in other towns, some as far away
as the Urals. Training was geared towards
the practical and included learning to use
the most diverse materials. The graduates of
the higher classes received the title 'artist-architect'. As designers at the drawing-board
and as consultants of manufacturing in workshops and factories they played a large part
in the development of a contemporary, modern culture of taste, not least in the field of
interior decoration.

Serial and mass production of everyday objects, at that time, however, was largely in the
hands of talented engineers, as well as those
working as employees of European companies in their Russian production firms. One

can therefore say that at the beginning of the
century the whole unity of craft and industrial
design in Russia was influenced from two
sides: by the inventive spirit of technicians
and designers, as well as by the attempts at
renewal within art and crafts which were to
become increasingly influential.

The situation had changed decidedly in at
least one aspect after the October Revolution
of 1917. Links with Western firms, which had
remained strong up until that point, were broken off. In many places the production of ne-
cessities slowed down. Textile production no
longer received pattern books from Paris. The
general economic situation of the country
began to stagnate. Anything that had gone before was rejected as 'bourgeois' and non-
contemporary while something new did not
yet appear to be in sight. At the same time, it
was precisely then that a new generation of
artists arose, amidst enormous social upheav-
al. They demanded the integration of art into
life and thus into the everyday by means of
leaflets, manifestos, catalogues, programmes
and lectures. Their appeals were so passion-
ately vehement and radical that the formal
language, inspired by French Cubism and
Italian Futurism, soon influenced the design of
everyday objects. The beginnings of this
avant-garde reached back to the pre-war
years. Kasimir Malevich had eliminated most
realistic elements from his painting as early as
1913. Two years later he showed his famous
Black Square on White Background at an exhibition in St Petersburg. This has long since
entered the history of Classical Modernism as
an incunablum of Suprematism which Male-

9

10

vich founded. At around the same time other Russian artists created their first abstract compositions. It was painters, stage designers and artistically trained designers such as Mikhail Larionov, Vladimir Tatlin, Natalia Goncharova and Alexander Rodchenko who welcomed the burgeoning political and social changes as an echo and confirmation of their own revolutionary spirit, and saw in them an all but unlimited possibility for future work. All the dreams contained in their early works, the initial stages of the Constructivism that would follow, appeared to be fulfilled under the Red Flag.

Abstraction, a consistent use of pure colours and forms, the rejection of traditional easel painting and the creative renewal of the world to which they wished to make a contribution were but a few of the priciples adhered to by the majority of young Russian artists. Some of their programmatic declarations and the majority of their works brought them close to Futurism. Many, however, reached beyond individual types of art by means of their utopian goals. The confidence with which they proclaimed their ideas had missionary qualities. 'Futurism described a new world of fast change and depicted the entire dynamics of contemporary life on the canvas . . . There is single-mindedness and everything on earth must be created with a purposeful form,' wrote Malevich in 1918.

Banning all realism from painting in favour of autonomy demanded a change in perception and a new understanding of art. Objects were broken up into single elements, into simple geometric forms and areas, into points, lines and structures. Instead of reproducing concrete, plastic forms by means of tones of colour, suggesting light and shadow, signs were created, attempting to reveal space and time, energy and movement. Sober visions of the future replaced the world that could be reproduced by using brushes and colours. Artists were fascinated by the possibilities suggested by science and technology, of overcoming huge distances by means of telegraphs, radio and air travel. In a letter to the composer, Mikhail Matiushin, Malevich enlarges upon the idea of making use of the earth and moon's gravity, dreaming of a time in which artists' studios and whole cities will be found on oversized space ships.

Despite numerous impulses from Western European art, the new 'isms' of the Russian avant-garde did not rest solely on mere repetition and imitation. Although one could initially find more or less recognisable references to the Cubism of Picasso and Georges Braque in individual works, such influences disappeared rapidly in the years after the October Revolution whose course followed its own rules in much the same way as the art that placed itself at its service. Creating something new was the primary and cardinal rule. This meant that painters, sculptors, architects and designers wished to break with all traditions, free themselves from all academic art and invent a manner of seeing and expressing themselves with its own system of reference, logic and ability to convince. Spatial constructions using minimal elements, such as those created by Rodchenko, had already become suffi-

11

9 Exterior of an agitatory aeroplane, 1920–21. – 10 Vinogradov: chair with hammer and sickle emblem, manufactured by MOSDREV for the House of the Peasant, 1922–23. – 11 Natan Altman: design for a 1-ruble stamp, 1920.

12

13

14

12 Agitatory porcelain, manufactured by the State Porcelain Factory in Leningrad, 1920–22. Plates by Michail Adamovitch, Sergei Tchechonin, Rudolf Wilde, Georgi Vyetchedchanin. – 13 Natan Altman: design for a 7-ruble stamp, 1920. – 14 *Detector* radio in ceramic case with inscription 'Listen to the newspaper without paper or cables', 1924.

15

cient to satisfy this demand. These were light plastic forms with an air of fragility that contradicted any previous ideas of volume and gravity, at the same time as having a hitherto unknown aesthetic attractiveness that even a critical observer could hardly deny.

On the other hand, it was the unusual aesthetic quality of huge buildings and the possibilities of technical achievements, the rhythm of machines and engines, the beauty of enormous space ships and bridges, that excited the sensibilities of the artists. They saw the realisation of their own ideas in the sobriety, rationality and disciplined austerity of technical forms. The decided inclination towards Constructivism and the use of anything that the technology of the time made possible (including concrete, glass and metal) displayed by Russian designers, largely derives from the confrontation with the functional aesthetic of architects and engineers. One is all too easily inclined to indentify the development of Russian art, as well as design, with big, well-known names and to overlook those young talents who, while still at the beginning of their development, identified with the proclaimed democratic ideals just as strongly. They rejected reactionary academic art and the idea of the petit-bourgeoisie as a public in just as decisive a manner. These artists, who were initially nameless, recognised a contract to renew the world and invent a new visual language amidst the social upheavals. Beyond this, they hoped for a larger circle of those interested in their art and for an increased understanding of consumption in those people who came into contact with artistically

created industrial products. Ignoring the trend towards using new stylistic methods, which had in mind the good of the public, things were still being produced in the traditional manner. Thus, allegorical subjects were used in agitative texts – images of factories, industrial chimneys and machines and, unavoidably, the emblems of the Soviet Union, appeared on postage stamps, all contrasting with the completely diverse system of expression using geometric and dynamic stylistic means with which the Russian artistic avantgarde believed it could fulfil the revolutionary spirit of the time.

The picture of design around 1920 is one-sided if one only measures it according to the achievements of the progressive faction who wished to renew it. Parallel to this ran a still large, conservative group, represented by those who, while belonging to the 'Intelligensia', inflexibly and unimaginatively clung to the use of traditional methods of design. Additionally, the numerous, often only short-lived, circles and groups formed by 'left-wing' artists regularly disagreed amongst themselves. Not only did their theses and programmes get caught up in contradictions, but also declared war on rival artists and artistic groups, even when their declared goals diverged only slightly from their own. One of the most obvious results of all attempts at reform on the part of the Russian avant-garde and its attempts to unite art and life was the interchangeability of art, sculpture, architecture and decorative arts. The borders of these genres increasingly began to blend into one another, so that traditional boundaries ac-

15 Suprematist tableware, manufactured by the State Porcelain Factory in Leningrad from 1922–23 with designs by Kasimir Malevich, Nicolai Suetin, Ilia Tchashnik.

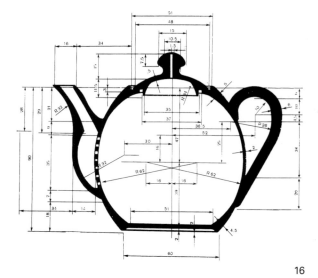

16

17

cording to formal criteria and exterior factors seemed difficult or hardly possible. A painting could acquire sculptural qualities, a sculpture could appear like an architectural model, a design for a textile pattern could seem to be an abstract composition and vice versa.

The dividing lines in artistic practice were versatile within related areas of work. Most art schools considered universality, in the sense of a training spanning various disciplines, a pedagogic ideal worth striving towards, whereby the autonomy of the budding artist became a multi-talented force counteracting the 'art specialist'. The great respect traditionally paid to the artist in Russia was increased by his working in various areas. Above all, a training that was as wide-reaching as possible, enriched by practical experience, made the cooperation of architects, sculptors, painters and designers on joint projects such as the Moscow artists' café 'Pittoresque' (1917–18) more simple (apart from the painter, designer and stage designer Vladimir Tatlin, Rodchenko, trained as painter and sculptor, Georgi Yakulov, who emerged mainly as a costume and stage designer, as well as several further artists who worked on this project). What united them was the fact that

they were convinced of the dawning of a new age with hitherto unforeseen possibilities for artistic freedom.

The necessity of defending this freedom *vis-à-vis* State institutions became apparent as early as 1917. Many artists regarded the plan to found a new ministry for fine arts, which was made shortly after the February Revolution, an attempt at State intervention. When the Bolsheviks took power a few months later, in October, even left-wing members of the avant-garde saw the autonomy of art in great danger. It was not until the end of 1918, when the Visual Arts Section in NARKOMPROS, the People's Commission for Cultural Education, was founded, and the nationwide founding of museums for modern art in the following year, that this danger appeared to abate – Malevich, Kandinsky, Tatlin and countless other exponents of Russian Modernism consciously placed their art at the disposal of the Revolution and identified with its message of renewing the world, even if this was not always their deepest convicton. 'We loudly praise the revolution as the primary impetus of life', proclaims the 'Manifesto of the Suprematists and Abstractionsts', written jointly by Rodchenko and Varvara Stepanova in 1919.

16 Alexei Filippov: design for a standardised tea-pot, 1928.
17 Vladimir Tatlin: beak-shaped cup for children (demonstration of how it is held), made according to instructions by Tatlin at the Ceramics Department of the VCHUTEMAS in Moscow.

18

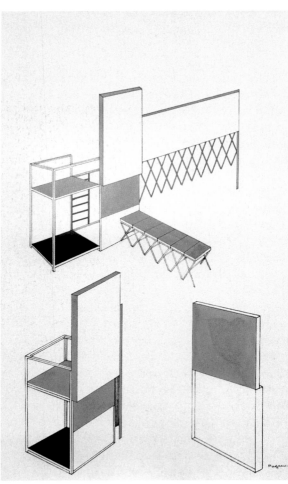

19

In the same year, the year the Comintern was founded, Vladimir Tatlin began his designs for the Monument to the Third International. The Monument, conceived as a construction made of glass and iron, was to reach higher than the Eiffel Tower and was to stand in the midst of a wide-reaching communication network. It was to contain a large conference room, with administrative and conference rooms, and, according to the technical possibilities available at the time, highly modern facilities that would receive news and spread propaganda. The entire object was to be surrounded by two intertwining spirals that became narrower towards the top, as did the stereometric building in the middle. While the lower space, surrounded by a cube, was to rotate completely once a year, Tatlin envisaged a monthly repeated rotation for the higher area. And lastly, the highest 'storey', a cylinder, was to turn around its own axis daily.

Like many Constructivist projects, Tatlin's tower was never realised. The model of this clear architectural vision, shown in 1920, has fired the imagination of countless architects and became in some ways symbolic of the enthusiasm for technology and the general feeling of change brought by those years. It once again expressed the aim of the artistic avant-garde to bring about a synthesis of all the arts, including architecture (which had its own department in the NARKOMPROS, although its advocates were rather conservative and tended to advocate Neo-classicism). Apart from Tatlin, it was mainly David Shterenberg who finally brought about a change in thinking at the People's Commission.

Further Russian painters left behind architectural designs in those years, for example Rodchenko's watercolour, dating from 1919, *House of the Apprentice*. Another work from the same period shows the view into an airport hall, consisting of an open metal construction above columns, between which move two human figures, reduced to basic geometrical shapes. Below the immense roof

18 Alexander Rodchenko: design for an overhead lamp in the Workers' Club at the Soviet Section of the 'International Exhibition' in Paris, 1925. – 19 Alexander Rodchenko: design for a convertible speaker's desk for the Soviet Section of the 'International Exhibition' in Paris, 1925.

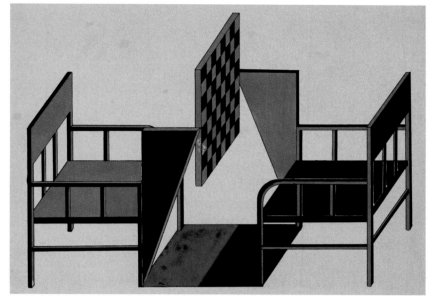

20

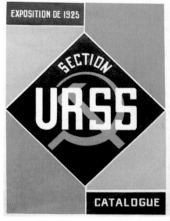

21

22

20 Alexander Rodchenko: design for a chessboard in the Workers' Club in the Soviet Section of the 'International Exhibition' in Paris, 1925. – 21 Alexander Rodchenko: design for the cover of the catalogue of the Soviet Section of the 'International Exhibition' in Paris, 1925. – 22 Interior of the Workers Club, built according to designs by Rodchenko, in the Soviet Section of the International Exhibition in Paris, 1925. Photo: Henri Manuel.

23

24

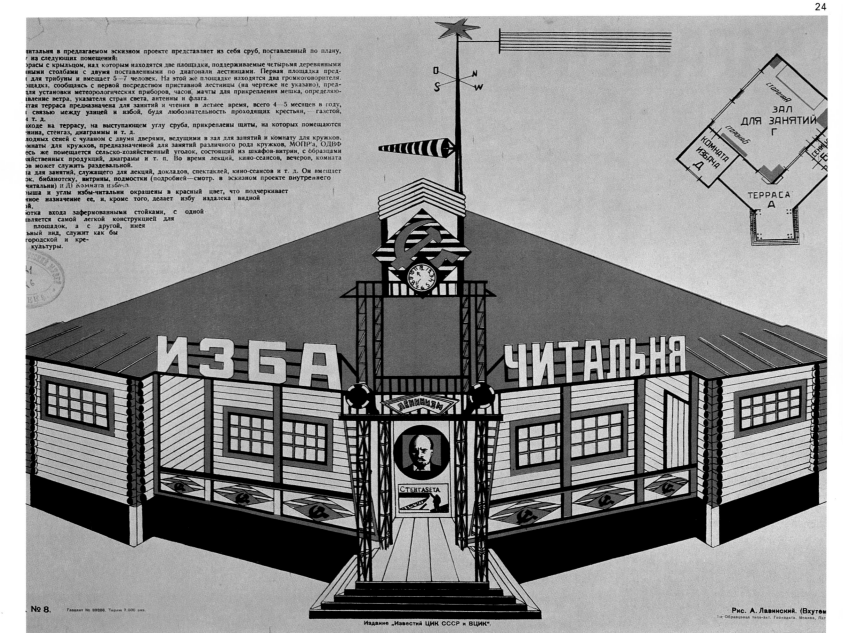

25

23 Meeting-room in a workers'
club in the twenties. – 24 Anton
Lavinski: design for a reading pavilion for farmers and peasants,
1925. The groundplan includes a
room for the librarian, another
for group meetings and a read-
ing-room (behind the entrance
terrace).

25 Yelena Semenova: design for
a club cantine, 1926. Inscription
over the bar: 'Healthy rest only in
the club'.

of the hall, they appear like schematic, ethere-
al creatures, abstracted assortments of limbs
in a metal labyrinth.

When the Communist International held its
Fourth Congress in Moscow in 1922, one of
the agitatorial works of art created by the
painter and designer Gustav Klutsis had con-
siderable public impact. This was a construction made of masts, struts and ropes which
supported posters, loudspeakers and book-
cases, installed on the roof of the delegates'
hotel.

Such art, used as an eye-catcher on streets,
squares and public parks, combined images
two-dimensionally as wall decorations, or as
physical constructions consisting of artistic
tools whose purpose was political en-
lightenment and instruction. The artist had to
constantly take into account the aesthetic and
psychological, as well as ideological, impact
of his work on the masses, whether in the
form of high speaker rostrums, frames for
projection screens or book and newspaper
kiosks; whether for the creation of festive
decorations for the square before the Winter
Palace in St Petersburg or whole street demonstrations in honour of the anniversary of
the victorious October Revolution. Art became
a means of propaganda. Simple stands for
selling things, diagrams and posters, even the
graphic design of food stamps thus became
instruments for political influence.

The signs that the era of unlimited artistic
freedom was coming to an end increased in
the year 1920. The periodical of the Futurists
had already folded up in the previous year, as
had *Iskusstvo,* the publication of the Department for Visual Arts in the People's Commission for Cultural Development. Likewise, the
professional body of painters, an organisation
that had distanced itself from any state intervention by governing itself, was disbanded.
Finally, in the winter of 1920/21, a wide-
reaching restructuring of the art section in
NARKOMPROS took place, after the Central
Committee of the Communist Party had level-
led hefty attacks specifically aimed at the
allegedly ideologically – unsound tendencies
amongst the Futurists. The question of the
artist's role in the newly forming society took
on ever greater urgency. The arguments
within the avant-garde and the individual
positions from which any of the rival factions
loudly proclaimed their ideas of the 'right'
way for contemporary art took place alongside economic problems, the hunger of the
masses and the mistakes made by technological, industrial modernisation of the country. In
the face of this situation, a change of course in
the ideal of artistic production free of ideology
appeared impossible. An important step in
this direction, also important for the development of industrial design, was the founding of
the Institute for Artistic Culture (INCHUK) in
Moscow in 1920, which was followed by the
opening of a branch in St Petersburg three
years later. The institute, at first headed by
Vassily Kandinsky and then by Rodchenko,
was devoted to research in art historical and
theoretic matters. A new term was making the
rounds at the time: production art. It arose
alongside the attempts made by a number of
INCHUK members to influence the production

26

27

methods for consumer goods with Constructivist concepts. The process of artistic creation and ordinary, everyday work was therefore assigned equal importance. They were not only trying to design objects clearly and functionally but were also attempting to make them as multi-functional as possible, aided by only a few movements of the hand (for example, Rodchenko stipulated that a bed could thus become a chair and that this could again be transformed into a desk). At VCHUTEMAS, the Higher State Art and Technology Workshops in Moscow (that had been created as a result of the amalgamation of the Stroganov School and the School of Painting, Sculpture and Architecture in 1918, from which the Free State Artists' Workshops or SVOMAS had arisen) this programme – developed largely by Constructivists – was put into practice. As a result of this increased tendency to work practically, at least part of the Russian avant-garde gained a new autonomy and became more conscious of its own identity. The gap between art and life became narrower and sometimes appeared to disappear altogether... ' This life, a simple thing, that one has up until now neither seen nor heard, that is so simple and clear that all one needs do is organise it and free it of all superfluous things,' wrote Rodchenko in 1921. He added that one should now 'work for the sake of life and not for palaces and temples, cemeteries and museums'.

The Paris Exhibition of 1925

After the Soviet Union had taken part in the Venice Biennale in the previous year, its participation in the Exposition internationale des arts décoratifs et industriels modernes (1925) in Paris provided the world at large with the opportunity to gain insight into the newest developments and trends in Russian art, particularly concerning new design methods within applied art.

A committee headed by Pavel Kogan and David Shterenberg had been formed at the end of 1924. The architect Alexander Poliakov was made responsible for designing the outer appearance of the Russian contribution to the Paris exhibition. An attempt was made to choose examples from aeroplane, railway and automobile construction from architecture, graphic art and book art, textile and furniture design, as well as from other crafts, that could be considered representative for the first phase of the Soviet Union and were worthy of being exhibited. Particularly great hopes were placed in the exhibition pavilion itself, as well as in a Workers' Club and Reading Room that were also to be shown.

In 1925, Ilia Ehrenberg praised the glass pavilion with its scaffold-like construction in the *Ekran* periodical: 'This is an industrial dream. A dream of an airport hall (must a poet always

26 Alexander Rodchenko: beer advertisement for Mosselprom (Moscow Industrial Organisation for Farm Products), 1925. 27 Metal box for Mosselprom products, mid-20s.

dream of tabernacles?) The glass rules out double meanings – it possesses the clearness of fair weather while simply being a simple window display case'.

The pavilion, designed by Konstantin Melnikov, proved to be a strong source of attraction. Apart from industrial products, it contained folk art and publications of the state publishers, amongst other objects. Isaak Rabinovich, who, together with Alexandra Exter, had designed the sets and costumes for the film *Aelita* (released in 1924), presented the literary exhibition as a reading room with comfortable chairs and tables, whereby anyone could take the book of his choice from the shelves. On the other hand, architectural exhibits, examples of advertising and poster art, home crafts and the State Porcelain Manufacturers, as well as particularly fine showpieces from the theatre were found at the Grand Palais.

Alexander Rodchenko's contribution to the Paris presentation by the burgeoning USSR consisted of, apart from his part in the designing of the pavilion, a row of single objects from urban and book design, applied graphic art and the project for the Workers' Club (on view in the Gallery of the Invalides Cathedral), one of the largest of all exhibits. The furniture was also fabricated in Paris, according to his designs. It was clearly important to Rodchenko to go further than presenting the club's social function as a leisure and educational centre for workers, exemplary for the state's great concern for the well-being of the proletariat. He also wished to demonstrate the courageous, imaginative and experimental spirit of an artistic generation that had decided to concentrate entirely on the future, helping Communist ideals to gain the upper hand. Rodchenko had conceived the club as a multifunctional space. This was mainly embodied by a moveable stage, which included a projection screen and a poster wall that could be pulled out. A podium could similarly be used to exhibit diverse objects, as well as for public speakers or lecturers. 'Living newspapers', scenic reproductions of contemporary events, were not unusual in Russia at the time.

Single objects were also multi-functional. Whilst the elements they were composed of could not be interchanged, they could indeed be altered: the beam of a lamp, the top of a reading table and the playing board of a chess table. As Rodchenko was himself an enthusiastic chess player, knowing the game's popular role in the life of ordinary people, it was no coincidence that part of his vast and manifold design work was for chess furniture and figures.

Rodchenko was honoured with a silver medal for his contribution to the Paris exhibition. It was not until sixty years of exhibiting his works at home and abroad had passed that it was decided to reconstruct Rodchenko's model of a workers club at the same spot in Paris. The attempt was successful – even the details of the complex embodied the Russian Constructivist style of the early twenties. The question of which structural characteristics and which outward circumstances in the postrevolutionary years influenced this style the most was raised, and not only by art historians and designers.

Its characteristics can be described in a precise fashion, as far as these are formal by nature. They appear in a somewhat diluted form in other artistic spheres, as in the costume and textile designs of Stepanova, or as in the first architectural projects of Konstantin Melnikov or the Vesnin brothers. The impression made by the most important elements is usually similar, whether on posters, books, agitative works of art or porcelain decoration. These are the basic geometric elements: the circle, square and right-angle (which was sometimes transformed into a simple Balkan cross, surrounded by simple or joint lines, or in the form of a sharply defined zig-zag). The expressivity of the single work of art depended less on the manner in which details were created than on the opposing tensions and directions of verticals and horizontals, light and dark, higher and lower, right and left. The mirrorings and breaks of geometric 'archetypes' also played an important compositional role and created optically ambivalent effects, surprises that caught one's gaze and confused at the same time, like picture puzzles.

The Soviet Union's participation in the Paris exhibition had wide-reaching consequences. Political isolation with all its economic consequences lessened, new trade connections were made, some information gaps were bridged and prejudices held abroad disappeared in the face of the well-chosen quantity of exhibited materials. The supposed mirror of real circumstances naturally remained silent about negative developments and hid contradictions, set-backs and deficiencies. This applied to the electrification of the USSR which was executed with a great deal of propaganda, as well as certain areas of metal and textile production. In these cases, as with the manufacture of simple, everyday furniture, production methods usually fell short of real demand. The willingess of manufacturers employed by the State to take advice from artists, let alone put this into practice, was all in all minor. There were, however, some exceptions. *Pravda* published an article by the chemo-technician of the First State Textile Company, P Viktorov. The author complained of the lack of co-operation between contemporary designers and the textile industry and stated that for this reason materials were still manufactured according to old patterns, dating from pre-revolutionary times. On the other hand, two artists had been supplying the Moscow factory with designs for years – Varvara Stepanova, Rodchenko's partner in both art and life, and Liubov Popova, who herself came from a family of textile manufacturers. Popova's death brought her work and post as professor at the VCHUTEMAS in Moscow to an untimely end. Viktorov's complaint could only be partially justified. On the one hand, a large part of the populace regarded the manufacture of textiles largely as an industry for creating durable working clothes; on the other hand, artists were neither particularly interested in making master designs, nor in selling these, and not at all in creating a fashion or encouraging a particular style. Varvara Stepanova, however, was an exception to the rule.

Stepanova's exhibits in Paris were only part of her many-faceted creative work which was to blossom towards the end of the twenties. Figurative – although linear – geometric compositions and theoretic essays about Con-structivist tasks and aims in the new Soviet society were followed by costume and set designs for the Meyerhold Theatre in Moscow, as well as by advertising posters, designs for sports clothing and a large number of typographic works. Only around twenty of the approximately 150 designs Stepanova presented at the First State Textile Factory were ever realised. This was but a meagre degree of success and throws light on the reluctance shown by designers to accept the eager offers on the part of artists. At the beginning, many were shocked by the new patterns, simply designed with a compass and ruler. Instead of the inevitable flower and plant decorations, they thought they could recognise certain elements apertaining to fence and railway line imagery, considered utterly unsuitable for female clothing.

Yet it is above all Stepanova who belongs to that avant-garde circle of male and female designers who wished to contribute actively to the method of production. They were not content to simply create designs but wished to play an active part in production plans, eager to decorate shops, work with specialised publications and oversee the production of their patterns. These wishes were only realised with difficulty, despite being sanctioned officially. At a conference of the LEF (Left Front of the Arts) in 1925, Ossip Bryk, a theoretician of production art, emphatically welcomed the attempts made by Constructivists to influence mass production and organise close cooperation between State factories and designers: 'The Zindel factory asked the Institute for Artistic Culture (INCHUK) what should be done to alter methods of production. The chosen path is the right one, not because it is concerned with textiles but because it deals with the whole relationship to production. Up until the present artists have taken no interest in methods of production. It did not occur to

28

29

30

31

32

28 Alexander Rodchenko: advertisement for *Ira* cigarettes with a text by Vladimir Mayakovsky, 1923, reconstructed by Varvara Stepanova in 1930. – 29, 30 and 31 Wrapping paper for caramels ('*Our Industry*') from the State Confectionary Factory *Red October*, texts by Nicolai Aseiev, 1924. – 32 Nicolai Sokolov: advertisement for chocolate, design for an industrial council in Odessa, 1924.

33

34

35

37

them that they should take into account the needs of the consumer and the technical possibilities of manufacturing rather than simply copying from books and albums'.

Increasingly bold design ideas could of course not counteract the long-standing lack of working clothes for the populace. Working suits for dockers, uniforms for pilots and protective clothing for miners or steel-workers, as well as functional and purpose-specific bags, buckles, belts and loops usually took conditions specific to the job into account. The concrete purpose influenced the form, yet the irony of history means that one often has to painstakingly reconstruct this kind of working clothing from single examples made for exhibitions.

38

39

Fashionable elegance was reserved mainly for the inhabitants of the large cities, as in Czarist times. Nadeshda Lamanova developed a pattern system that could cleverly hide obesity or bring out single shapes by means of appropriate draping. The secret lay in the right-angled cut of the material from which the dress was to be made: 'in order to achieve the best design of a piece of clothing, one must take the given shape apart, creating geometric forms in order to make the actual silhouette clearer', Lamanova proclaimed. 'In projecting this silhouette onto a plane one must understand it as if it consisted of a number of single parts. If these are not in harmony with one another the individual parts must be changed in order to achieve a greater harmony in the relationship of the parts with each other and therefore also in the finished dress'.

33 Alexander Rodchenko: advertisement for *Dobrolet* with the appeal to become a shareholder in the Society for the Development of Aeronautics, 1923. – 34 *Dobrolet* exhibition pavilion at the 'First Federal Russian Exhibition for Farming and Crafts' in Moscow, 1923. – 35 Alexander Rodchenko: *Dobrolet* emblem, 1923.

36 Andrei Andreyev: emblem for the Harmony Company, mid-1920s. – 37 Andrei Andreyev: emblem for the 5th Printing-House in Moscow, mid-1920s. – 38 Sachar Bykov: emblem for the State Metalworks, 1924. – 39 Andrei Andreyev: advertisement for wood storage, mid-1920s.

40

41

Nadeshda Lamanova was also represented in the special supplement that the periodical *Krasnaia Niva* brought out. The publication depicted many examples of her work and large, handsome reproductions of speakers' tribunes, theatre designs, club furniture and clothing. Amongst these, designed by Lamanova, was a sport suit, a teacher's uniform (the armless clothing of Russian peasant women, buttoned in front), a dress made from material usually worn as a headscarf, and a 'Tolstoika' which is a wide shirt worn over trousers with a belt Tolstoy enjoyed wearing (it is also named after him). What is noteworthy about these pieces is that one could make them according to pattern from relatively easily obtainable materials. Without attempting to be fashionably extravagant, they were aimed more at the average citizen, who was used to overcoming material difficulties by improvisation and self-help when faced with a lack of choice. A few years later the *Jungsturm* became popular. This was a sporty, military outfit, rather like a pilot's uniform. In this case it was the *Kamsomolskaia Pravda* that advised its young readers to make it themselves and with great success, as it turned out.

42

40 and 41 Alexei Gan: Vserokompom (Russian Council for Manufacturing Industry) sales stand for books and paper, view of the kiosk, open and closed, 1924. – 42 Anton Lavinsky: book kiosk at the Theatre Square in Moscow, 1925.

43

44

The Soviet Union had painted a positive and even enticing picture of its economy in the Paris exhibition of 1925. The evidently rapid growth of consumer goods production was shown to be of central importance, part of the general theme of the transformation of a backward agricultural country into a modern industrial state. Even if they ignored all propagandistic exaggerations, visitors could gain the impression that this process was being aided by the most creative forces in the country of their own accord and with exemplary vigour. The latter was certainly the case and remained so for the next years. It was a fact, however, that it was not only lack of materials and bureaucratic, ideological problems that made the introduction of new methods of production difficult, thus having negative effects on product design (not to mention demand in comparison to what was on offer). It was much more the conservative taste of the masses that proved to be a hindrance. In the textile industry of the following years, where the level of production only reached pre-war

levels around 1927, one increasingly reverted to figurative design. Aeroplane, machine and sports patterns replaced abstract designs. At the same time both designers and manufacturers were fully aware that the majority of potential customers still favoured traditional textile designs with leaf and flower patterns.

The discussions about the future path of textile design that took place amongst designer collectives, professional bodies and decision-makers of large, state factories in the late twenties were characterised by heated arguments about details in the design of decorative elements appropriate for the times (or what was considered appropriate), as well as uncertainty and pragmatic opportunism. A similar phase of change, whereby a younger generation was questioning previous design methods and forms, could also be found in other areas of the decorative arts. The end of avant-garde design in Russia was close at hand.

43 A Rybnikov: emblem of the State Publishing House Gosizdat, 1924. – 44 Varvara Stepanova with the cap, manufactured according to her designs, for the booksellers of the State Publishing House Gosizdat, 1924.

45

46

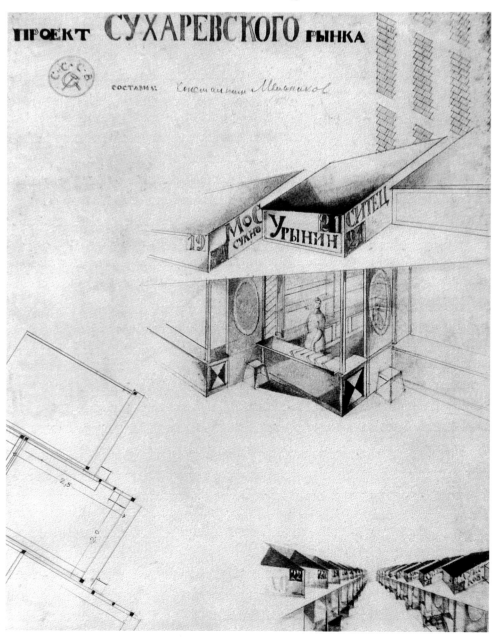

ПРОЕКТ СУХАРЕВСКОГО РЫНКА

составил: Константин Мельников

45 The Sucharevsky Market in Moscow after construction was completed, 1928. – 46 Alexander Rodchenko: advertising board for confectionary on the roof of a Mosselprom kiosk in Moscow, 1924. Photo: A Rodchenko. – 47 Konstantin Melnikov: drawings for the design of the Sucharevsky Market in Moscow, 1924.

47

The Role Played by the Art Schools

When Lenin signed the 'Decree of the Peoples Commissioners Council concerning the Higher State Art and Technology Workshops in Moscow' at the end of 1920, the VCHUTEMAS had been in existence for two years, although not under this name. Their founding resulted from the merging of the former Stroganov Art School and the earlier Art, Sculpture and Architecture School, known as the Second Free State Art Workshops (SVOMAS) after the Revolution, in the wake of the general educational reforms of 1918.

What differentiated the VCHUTEMAS from all previous art institutions was not merely the rejection of academic methods of learning and the conscious practice of a widely democratic educational system with a training spread through eight faculties. Of greater consequence was the fact that three further principles were put into practice: objective analysis of form that the compulsory basic course taught all students; the removal of hierarchical order in the artistic disciplines with a corresponding equality of all subjects as well as, finally, a practical training that was geared towards social needs and aimed at widening the influence of what was subsumed under the title of 'production art' at the end of the twenties. The fact that artists such as Kandinsky and Rodchenko, Tatlin and El Lissitsky, as well as countless other prominent members of the avant-garde taught at the VCHUTEMAS explains the great influence this school (comparable to the German Bauhaus) had on art theory and, even more strongly, on almost all areas of Russian art of the twenties.

The development of design in the period after the Revolution is hardly imaginable without the impulses made by the VCHUTEMAS. Its educational goals coincided with the aims of the textile, wood and metal industry as well as the production plans of ceramic and glass factories. Rodchenko, who taught at VCHUTEMAS for ten years (he had been Dean of the Metalwork Factory since 1922) expected his students to 'realise the artistic, technological goals of our time by means of concrete work with the materials'. For this one needed the ability to combine the fuctions and form of an object in a practical and, at the same time, aesthetically pleasing manner, using one's own creativity and knowledge of materials.

This was a skill many VCHUTEMAS graduates excelled in. El Lissitsky, who had been made head of the architectural faculty as early as 1921, returned to Moscow after a prolonged stay in Berlin in 1925 in order to take up a post at the VCHUTEMAS. The respect he earned was based on his close cooperation with Malevich at the Vitebsk Art School where he had been taught by Marc Chagall, and his architectural experience and his activities in UNOVIS – a group of artists who single-mindedly defended the idea of workers' collectives, developed new forms of street and agitative art and developed energetic initiatives to reform art education.

Lissitsky succeeded in communicating this wish for renewal to his students. A series of furniture designs, in which the search for basic forms in the sense of standardisation can easily be discerned, was developed under his aegis. Lissitsky's architectural projects and, more importantly, his plans for the interior decoration of communal apartments, repeatedly adopt the idea of standardised norms and patterns. He believed that apartments should be as sparsely furnished as ships' cabins or railway compartments. Along with his students, he designed a two-storey apartment in which chairs were conceived as mobile furniture. As early as 1923 Lissitsky advocated flexible dividing walls in an essay. These were to correspond to changing household needs and were to be used as elements to divide space.

At a conference of the Council of the Peoples Commissionaries in 1928, Lissitsky, still as VCHUTEMAS Professor for Interior Design, held a lecture on the artistic prerequisites for the standardisation of individual pieces of furniture. Today, this still reads like a paradigm of all manifestos, programmes and resolutions in which the leaders of the Russian avant-garde defined their idea of 'artistic freedom'. According to Lissitsky, five basic principles had to be adhered to for all objects to be used in the home:

'1. They represent themselves and nothing further. THEY ARE HONEST.

2. The eye need not wander over them and become distracted by complex forms. THEY ARE CLEAR.

3. They are simple and energetic. THEY ARE ELEMENTARY.

4. One can design the whole object, as well as detail, by using a ruler and compass.

5. They are produced by man with the help of machines. THEY ARE INDUSTRIAL.'

Vladimir Tatlin, in the meantime also known abroad for the Monument for the Third International, only arrived at the school in 1928, which had been renamed the VCHUTEIN (Higher State Institute of Art and Technology) the previous year. The fact that he taught woodwork and ceramics in Moscow, after being head of the department of photo, film and theatre at the Kiev Art School from 1925–27, as well as working as a theatre director, set designer and actor, betokens the universality of this man's creativity (in the thirties he was officially disgraced and spent the last decade of his life working at uninspiring odd-jobs). He aligned himself with the teaching programme of the VCHUTEMAS-VCHUTEIN in his belief that art should develop models for technical appliances and banal, but necessary everyday objects. While studying the aesthetic qualities of materials, his class designed objects made from glass, wood and metal. Amongst these were steel tube chairs and 'Letatlin' (1929–32), a one-seat, curved steel flying machine, reminiscent of a sledge. 'While manufacturing an object, the artist has a whole range of diverse materials at his disposal whose characteristics in the areas of colour, workability, malleability and durability he must take into account', commented Tatlin on his students' designs in 1929.

At the time, however, Tatlin's explanation can hardly have appeared original. It was more of a summary of the work of previous years, of the delight in formal experimentation in the workshops (as can be seen in photographs and other documents), as well as of the argument between followers of traditional design and left-wing Constructivists. On the other hand, initial reformatory enthusiasm had markedly weakened at the time of Tatlin's arrival at the school. It had given way to a more pragmatic, one-sided training, concentrating on technical innovation that helped the new profession of designers to come into existence. From 1927-29 it was possible to gain diplomas from various classes in the metal and woodwork faculties. An example of the demands made on the VCHUTEIN graduates of the time can be seen in the design for a vehicle for un-navigable ground, softened by rain and melt-ed snow. Another work consisted of plans for a railway engine with additional compartments for goods, passengers, sanitary facilities and sleeping compartments; in the case of another construction, students attempted to create multi-purpose exhibition buildings.

Standardisation and purpose-oriented design of form was the vocabulary of those interested in renewal and reform at Russian art schools in the twenties and was almost identical with that used by art educators, architects and designers in the West to programmatically set out their aims. Both were interested in developing industrially-produced consumer products that were as functional as possible.

As far as Russia is concerned, it is not only VCHUTEMAS-VCHUTEIN that contributed to the creation of a new idea of design in a major way (thanks to the methods of analysing form which were part of the study programme and teaching by well-known members of the avant-garde). Important inspiration for this also came from other schools and their workshops. The former Free Art School in St Petersburg (then Petrograd) was incorporated by the VCHUTEMAS in 1921. This was at about the same time as the opening of the State Institute for Artistic Culture (INCHUK), where two years later, Malevich was appointed the Head and where Tatlin also worked. Although this institute was primarily concerned with artistic theory (Malevich liked comparing it to a laboratory) at least the experimental work, such as the attempt to bring formal elements from the new painting into architecture, had a similar influence on art in the early twenties as the INCHUK in Moscow which was founded at the same time. It was here that the theoretic basis for Constructivism was conceived, predominantly by Rodchenko.

The Art Workshop of the Working Youth (ISORAM), founded in St Petersburg in 1925 – which also had a branch in Moscow – had more modest aims than the VCHUTEMAS with its courses for young lay talents from the working classes. And yet, it mobilised as yet undiscovered talents with new teaching methods. It succeeded in achieving a great deal with increasingly Constructivist formal elements by producing stage, poster and book designs, artistic agitation in the form of wall paintings and street decorations, as well as furniture designs.

48

49

48 Hall in the Moscow Department Store No 1, 1928. – 49 Yelena Semenova: display window design for the perfume manufacturer TEDCHE, 1926.

50

51

The emergence of Socialist Realism at the beginning of the thirties resulted in the termination of the activities of ISORAM. Years before, in 1923–24, the 'leaders' of Constructivism, the aforementioned INCHUK, had to be closed, due to the withdrawal of state funding. This was soon to be the fate of further institutes, schools and groups. The results of their work, however, could not be wiped out by self-imposed or state-commissioned closings, especially as it had found international recognition at the latest in 1925, the year of the Paris exhibition. The fact that arguments about programmes and methods, envy, self-over-estimation and blind ambition hastened the end of one or the other school or artistic group, does not narrow their achievement as a whole, nor their public impact. Kandinsky's withdrawal from the INCHUK, which he co-founded, is therefore only one example of many. His leaving was linked to the increasing power of the 'Objective Analysis Group' and its concepts, which had been formulated under Rodchenko's aegis.

These ideas culminated in the attempt at developing objective criteria for art. Of primary importance – at least theoretically – was linking art and technology, image and construction, practically placing them side by side. One member of the group, the architect Nicolai Ladovski, stated that 'the technical construction is a combination of given materials with specific planning schemes aimed at achieving stronger effects'. The 'objective analysts' all believed that their ideas should be realised in 'real things and real rooms'. The fascination that technology had for many artists of the first avant-garde generation is mirrored in the titles and themes of many of their written statements. 'In earlier times engineers used art as relaxation', Rodchenko noted around 1922, 'while today artists use technology to recuperate'.

There is hardly an area of art, whether fine or decorative, including film and photography, that was not influenced by the consciously simple, effective, clear style of the Constructivists. This included abstract spatial constructions and architectural projects, and theatre productions in streets, squares and factory buildings, where costumes were often similar to ordinary working clothes and furniture designs of the kind seen in the interior of the workers' club at the Paris exhibition. All superfluous, decorative elements disappeared from

52

50 Varvara Stepanova: sportive dress, designed 1923, resewn by Yelena Chudyakova in 1986. – 51 Liubov Popova: actor's costume for a production of *The Generous Cuckold* by F Crommelynk at the Mayerhold Theatre in Moscow, 1922. – 52 Liubov Popova: dress design, 1923.

53

54

55

53 Varvara Stepanova: material
design, 1924. – 54 Varvara Stepanova: sportive dress, 1923, resewn by Yelena Chudyakova in
1986. – 55 Varvara Stepanova:
material design, 1924.

stage designs in favour of strongly expressive elements. There was a surprising degree of functionality and geometrically-structured patterning in the form and decoration of ceramic articles. Advertising lost its usual look with the advent of Constructivist methods. This included advertisements and posters, typeface and books, all areas of applied graphic art, from large agitatory posters to printed sweet wrappers.

One of the aims most strongly advocated by the Revolution was to put an end to illiteracy (found above all in the rural areas during the Czarist era). Therefore, the printing media of the early Soviet Union had an enormous task (alongside the reorganisation of schooling and the enactment of other public means of education). Advertising for books, for new educational possibilities, including primary level reading and writing, was usually in the form of posters and diagrams on kiosks, as well as in newspapers and leaflets. State publishing houses published illustrated periodicals, literature and socially critical books with large editions. Extensive and comprehensive production demanded high-quality graphics with effective methods, as well as smooth organisation. Therefore, the State publisher GOSIZDAT planned a number of book kiosks in Moscow, a refurbishing of bookshops (mainly their window displays), and street selling, as well as creating bookshops and a uniform for employees. Striking advertising was encouraged to draw attention to new publications. Declamatory eye-catchers such as arrows, exclamation marks, oversized capital letters and banner headlines within the text allowed the graphic design of books and covers to appear like small posters.

Designs for kiosks demonstrated that one could fold out doors and windows in order to achieve display space that was as large as possible. Only Anton Lavinski's ideas were realised, although there were numerous projects of this kind by Rodchenko, Gustav Klutsis, Grigori Miller and others. The artists' attempts at creating new, effective advertising did not fail completely (they also succeeded in designing all GOSIZDAT shops with the company colours of black, gold and red) – the

capital letters, typical of poster art in the twenties, attracted potential customers, especially those interested in art, as it was artists that had developed this typography with compositions made up of single letters and words, bringing it to a wider public.

This advertising, also observed with interest abroad after the Paris exhibition, promoted the most diverse objects with elements that constantly reoccurred – for example, it encouraged the buying of schoolbooks, galoshes or babies' dummies in the Moscow GUM department store. Portraits of state and party functionaries even greeted one from wrapping paper and confectionary boxes. 'Advertising must always remind one of wonderful things', Vladimir Mayakovski wrote in 1923. 'We must not leave this weapon to the followers of the NEP (New Economic Policy) or the foreign bourgeoisie . . . Think about advertising!'

Mayakovski was one of the few poets and writers in the Soviet Union of that time who consciously placed the power of words at the service of both political agitation and advertising. In 1923–24 he created hundreds of interesting, partly rhyming texts for the Moscow department store MOSSELPROM, the MOSPOLYGRAF printing house, the GOSIZDAT printing house and further large state firms who produced bread or biscuits and other foods, as well as beer, cigarettes, pencils and even fire-extinguishing hoses. The designs by Rodchenko, Varvara Stepanova, Anton Lavinski and A Levin heightened the effectiveness and thus the advertising qualities of the texts. 'An educated man will improve farmwork', reads the text of a poster from 1925 designed jointly by Mayakovski and Stepanova.

Production design of things advertised publicly did not of course always demonstrate the generally high level of aesthetic design elements that had emerged in poster and advertising art. Lack of materials and technical possibilities, as well as considerations of usefulness and the arguments about form and taste, again and again placed limits on industrial production of goods and their distribution. Under these circumstances, compromises in production were inavoidable.

56

56 Andrei Andreyev: Badge of the Association of Sewers, 1925.

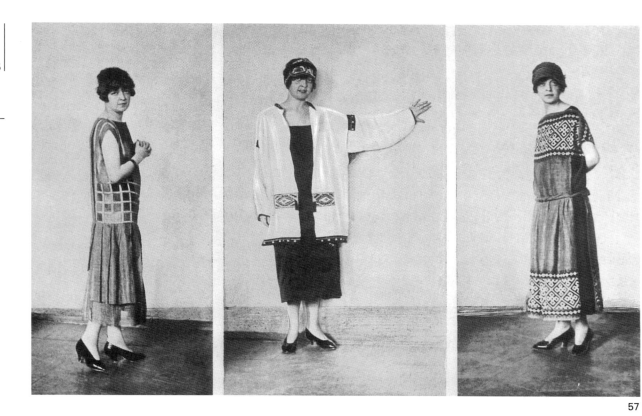

57

58

57 Fashion studio Nadeshda Lamanova: female clothing with contemporary folkloric patterns, 1924–25. – 58 Alexandra Exter: designs for dresses, coats and accessories, 1923.

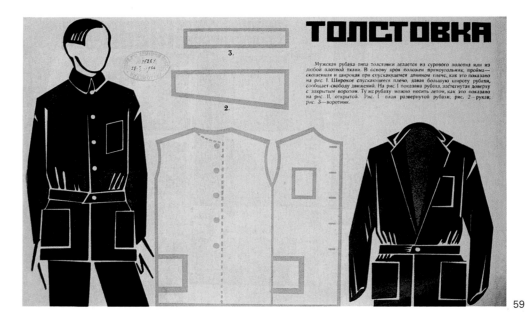

ТОЛСТОВКА

Мужская рубаха типа толстовки делается из сурового полотна или из любой плотной ткани. В основу кроя положен прямоугольник, пройма — скошенная и широкая при спускающемся длинном плече, как это показано на рис. I. Широкое спускающееся плечо, давая большую широту рубахи, сообщает свободу движениям. На рис. I показана рубаха, застегнутая доверху с закрытым воротом. Ту же рубаху можно носить летом, как это показано на рис. II, открытой. Рис. I — план развернутой рубахи; рис. 2 — рукав; рис. 3 — воротник.

59

60

The first competitions for serial mass production of furniture were held in the early twenties. Several basic demands were made: furniture should be easy to handle, weigh little, have the ability to be folded, be upholstered in a simple, cost-effective manner. In 1921, a collection of essays entitled 'Art in Production' was published by the People's Commission for Cultural Education. The authors advocated close cooperation between artists and State companies. Three years later, the publication *Art and Industry* published a row of furniture designs, resulting from competitions amongst designers. Most of the furniture one could buy at the time did not distinguish itself by particularly attractive forms. On the whole, it appeared clumsy and heavy. More intricate pieces often had factories or Soviet emblems as decorative elements. The *Album of Drawings and Furniture Designs* by P Duplitzky and K Musselius from Leningrad, published in 1929, demonstrates that there were attempts to create links between craft conventions and modern 'objectivity' in the twenties, alongside the attempt to create a consciously functional design of furniture. It is similar to a sample book for carpenters and handymen. The designs and models in the book demanded only simple fabrication and production. Only a minor amount of furniture had decorations. Clear, noticeably modest forms dominate, although reproduction of traditional furniture, chairs with bent legs, wide double beds with headrests, and side tables for hotels, were included. The idea of multi-purpose, space-saving furniture, which Rodchenko propagated and exhibited by means of practical examples at the Paris exhibition, took effect.

61

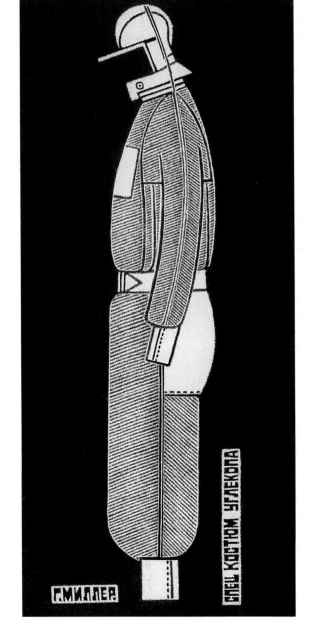

62

Overcrowded living conditions in the large cities and newly created industrial centres near these, actually forced people to use this poly-functional furniture to a greater extent. The engineer and artist, Ivan Lobov, showed a room for two to three people with purpose-built furniture at an exhibition of the VCHU-TEIN faculty for wood design in Moscow in 1929. Lobov wrote in an article ('Rationalised furniture for one-room apartments') that the lack of apartments meant 'that an apartment should be contained in a single room'. The designer had to take these conditions into account to solve the problem of space in the most effective manner possible. Therefore Lobov's design included beds and tables that could be folded, as well as a cupboard on various levels in which one could raise and then lower clothes. Using space in the most effective manner possible, all the furniture was contained in 16.35 square metres and a bedroom could be converted into a dining-room and then into a workroom; with screens dividing the room.

The aesthetic quality of much of the furniture dating from this period, even if it remained at the design stage, has roots in concrete material factors. Aside from the situation of the market and the wishes of the consumers, interior decorators were confronted by a great housing crisis. Designers were almost forced to invent new types of furniture. They needed to go beyond a simple lack of decoration or comfortable sizes (leading to standardisation).

Artists' collectives, design schools and factory design offices were therefore all the more in-

59 Nadeshda Lamanova: *Tolstovska* jacket, drawing by Vera Muchina, 1925. – 60 Varvara Stepanova: day dress, designed in 1924, resewn in 1986 by Yelena Chudiakova.

61 Vladimir Tatlin in his new 'rationalistic' menswear, wearing an all-purpose coat and a suit, 1923. In the background is the energy-saving oven that Tatlin developed at the Department of Material Culture at the State Institute for Artistic Culture in Leningrad. – 62 Grigori Miller: design for protective clothing for miners, 1924.

ЧАРЛИ ЧАПЛИН,

ВЕСЕЛЫЙ

АМЕРИКАНЕЦ,

Его показывают на картинах в кино,
Решил представить путешествие на экране,—
И для этого объехать шар земной.
Везде побывать… на все взглянуть,—
Решил, надел котелок—и в путь.

— 4 —

Но поскорее объехать весь свет как?
Чарли Чаплин и тут не сплошал.—
У Чарли Чаплина

МОТОЦИКЛЕТКА

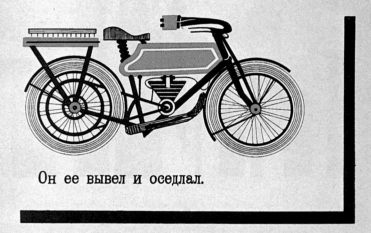

Он ее вывел и оседлал.

Все замелькало, как в кино,
Город остался за спиной.

— 5 —

63

64

63 Galina and Olga Chichagova:
Charlie's Journey, drawings for a
book about Chaplin's journey
around the world for children,
text by Leonid Smirnov, 1925. –
64 Unknown designer: *Work and
Capital,* kinetic toy, 1920s.

terested in public discussion of their work. Exhibitions, sometimes in theatres or cinemas, as well as articles in newspapers and periodicals aided this, sometimes leading to the realisation of a design. The aforementioned workshops of the Leningrad ISORAM had some success in this respect. The experimenting young workers, led by independent engineers and artists created monumental and poster art or stage and club design, as well as furniture design. The WOODTRUST exhibition in Leningrad presented several examples, including benches, buffet tables and clothes stands.

Difficulties arose, less during design than during production of essential consumer goods, in the textile, furniture and household appliance industries. They were undoubtedly even more apparent in industrial spheres of the USSR such as in machine construction and electricity production, which were forerunners of the general modernisation of the country. Foreign imports alone could not bring about technological progress. Instead, one looked at examples from Western production and then more or less accurately took over the exterior form. A large number of original, high-level creations were created. The small tractors, Karlik and Gnom, constructed in the Voroshdenie factory by J Mamin are examples. They were so easy to manoeuver that farmers told the manufacturers that they could be used effortlessly and without any instructions.

A similarly miraculous effect in the sphere of transport was created by the four-seater NAMI-1. This was the first vehicle for private transport constructed completely by the Scientific Research Institute for Automobiles and Engines. The Ja-6 bus of the Jaroslav car factory was developed in 1928-32 after the British Leyland model. The chassis and engines were transported to Moscow where construction of the bodywork of wood or metal and the assembling of the parts took place.

Further developments with favourable perspectives could be found in aeronautics. The ANT-1 aeroplane was developed in the Central Aero-Hydrodynamic Institute in 1921 and was soon the primary model for inland machines that could be used for long flights. They were the only means of transport within the huge Soviet empire that could also reach the north when the biennial impassability of country

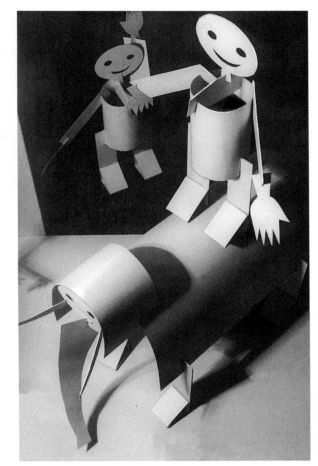

65

65 Alexander Rodchenko and Varvara Stepanova: *Circus,* photograph of cardboard figures, constructed according to principles of standardisation, 1926.

66

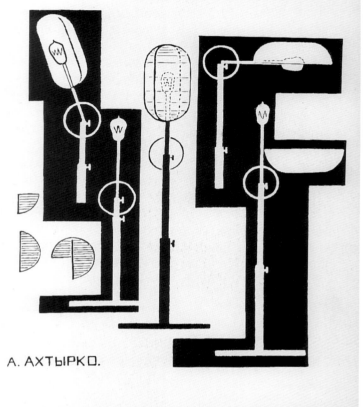

ПРОЭКТ ЛАМПЫ.

А. АХТЫРКО.

67

68

66 Sachar Bykov: design for tiles, 1922. – 67 Anastasia Akhtyrko: design for a (convertible) standing lamp, 1922. – 68 Sachar Bykov: model of an ashtray. The ash is poured into the interior of the pyramid by means of the triangular areas at the sides.

69 and 70 Ivan Morozov: universal table which can be converted into a work or dining table (tablecloth, plates and chairs are stored inside). – 71 Sachar Bykov: VCHUTEMAS emblem for May 1st, 1924. – 72 Alexander Galatnikov: diploma construction, model of a standard exhibition space, made of tubes, metal and wooden panels, 1929.

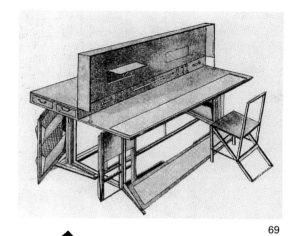

69

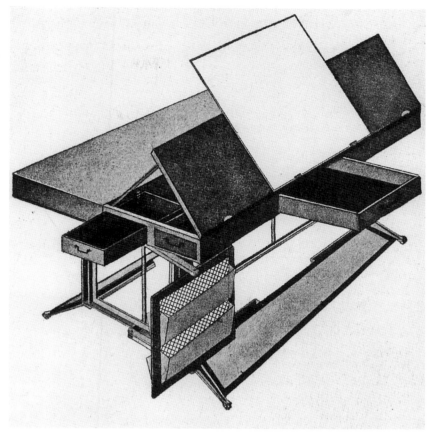

70

71

72

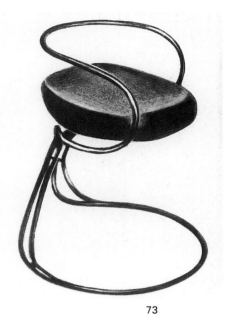

73

74

75

76

73 Rogoshin: chair with metal tubes, 1928, VCHUTEMAS Department of Woodwork, headed by Vladimir Tatlin. – 74 Nicolai Sokolov building a model of a cupboard door between kitchen and dining room that can be reached from both sides. Semester design in the class of El Lissitsky, 1928. Photo: A Rodchenko. – 75 Boris Semlianizin: folding chair, part of a diploma with designs for the interior of a captain's cabin, 1928. – 76 Workshop of the *Proletkult* Group: chairs that can be converted to tables by folding the back, 1925.

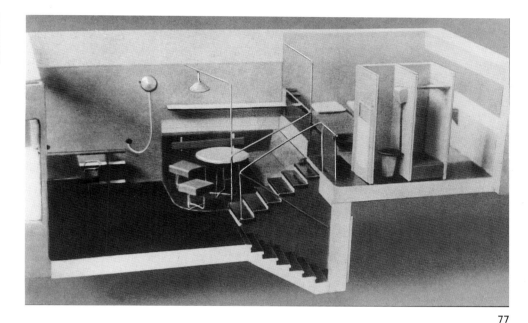

77

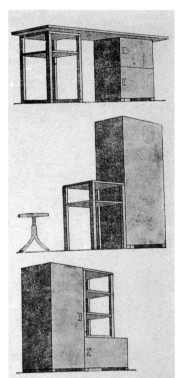

78

roads made all other reliable transport methods impossible. The AVTODOR (Automobile and Traffic Institute) was in some ways in competition with the Central Aero-Hydrodynamic Institute (TZAGI).

A photo, dating from 1824, depicts the ANT-5, developed by Andrei Tupolev, in Red Square, Moscow. There were aeroplanes of this type with open and closed cabins (for passengers). During construction, corrugated aluminium sheets had been tested, a material that was to become technically viable later with the Maxim Gorki. On the other hand, the first Russian planes constructed entirely from metal were bought from the German Junkers-Werke in 1923 for the inland airline, DOBROLET. This was one of the first firms for which Alexander Rodchenko designed emblems, advertising posters and even cufflinks for their test flights (1923–25). In the late twenties, DOBROLET (State Joint-Stock Company for the Promotion of Aeronautics) had as many as 20,000 passengers a year on the Moscow-Nishni and Moscow-Ivanov route. The names P Strakhov, M Kirpitshev, W Engelmeier, I Rerberg and V Shukhov are linked to the design of trains and transport machines, constructed in the initial phases of the emergence of technology in Russia (which was to grow rapidly). They usually preferred light, open and flexible constructions and therefore reacted to the demands of the ever-growing transport industry. In the case of a diesel lock, designed by Yakov Gakkel in 1924 in Leningrad, the driver's compartment was separated from the machine room. Such improvements resulted from experiences that were also used for local auto-

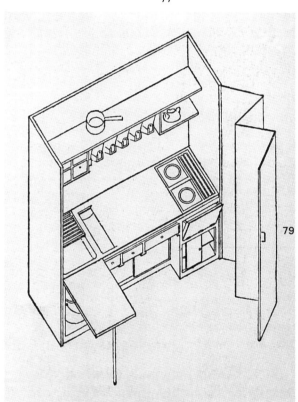

79

77 El Lissitsky: model of the Type F interior of the one-family appartment designed by Mosei Ginsburg, consisting of one-and-a-half rooms, 1929. – 78 El Lissitsky: design for combination furniture, 1929–30. – 79 Lisgor: design for a kitchen, 1929.

80

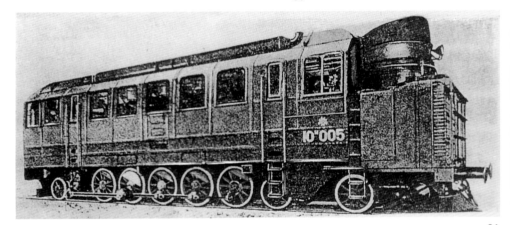

81

mobile construction (but not where foreign models provided inspiration or whole production facilities were imported). The interior of the AVTOGIGANT automobile factory in Nishni Novgorod, formerly Gorki, came from America. This factory built cars and lorries imitating Ford models in its first five years, 1928–32, although adapting them to local conditions.

If one includes the last six or seven years of the Czarist regime as being part of the period in which Russian design and industrial design gained importance with the help of the artistic avant-garde and increasingly influenced the cultural and economic development of the Soviet Union (being a largely independent discipline at State educational institutions), one can easily distinguish the achievements of three generations. The first, to which Kandinsky, Malevich, Tatlin, Rodchenko, Varvara Stepanova and others belonged, created the theoretical and practical basis (with their abstract formal experiments) for the second generation which mainly adhered to Constructivism. Many members of this middle generation had received their education at the VCHUTEMAS, not completing the course and going straight into practical work. This included Grigori Miller, A Akhtyrkov, Yelena Semenova and the sisters Galina and Olga Chichagova. Therefore, the third generation, after being educated at the VCHUTEMAS-VCHUTEIN,

82

83

avidly took over the many tasks of design in all areas of industrial production as well as in theatre, film, public transportation and architecture. Amongst the most well known of these were Sachar Bykov, Ivan Morosov, Vladimir Pavlov, Alexander and Piotr Galaktionov and Abram Damski.

The spiritual vision and actual heritage (in visible examples of their work) of these three generations did not decrease in the years of the formalism discussion and State regimentation of artistic life. The aims of the primary and consolidatory phases of Russian design, influenced by concrete social needs, remained alive in the imagination of the people. Although there was some agreement in the matter of form, design tasks were different to those in the West. Workers' clubs, book kiosks and working clothes were being designed, not opera houses, garden huts or elegant evening wear. The largest target group of Russian designers was the working people, not the wealthy élite.

84

80 Design office by Andrei Tupolev: Ant-5 sled with propellor on Red Square in Moscow, 1924. – 81 Diesel locomotive with magnetic friction sheet, late 1920s. – 82 AMO F-15 lorry, constructed 1924–31 (modelled on the Fiat) in the Moscow Carworks.

83 NAMI-1, the first Soviet lightweight car, double doors, 1927. – 84 The DM-1 glider is transported to the Moskva. Photo: A Rodchenko.

2 DESIGN AND SOCIETY

86

Design and Society

With the methods of applied art we will bring about the active ideological class war, we will renew life, increase the quality of industrial production and improve the taste of the working classes.
P Novitski

87

The artistic independence of Russian design in the twenties was replaced by an increasing lack of freedom in formal matters in the period following. This was due to the wishes and ideologically-motivated demands of the political leadership. It was not only art, but the entire body of culture that was to succumb.

The manufacture of industrial products, including the traffic and transportation methods used at the time, developed in accordance with what was expected of the rapid process of modernisation which also dominated the industrial development of other countries. Already in the twenties, however, there was an increased need for generalised standards in production. More attention was now paid to the durability of products. Aerodynamic laws were also paid greater attention if they could be of use in the development of new models. Household appliances, lamps and furniture changed their exterior appearance with the use of synthetic materials (bakalite, celluloid, plexiglass) and metals received protective coatings made of nickel and chrome.

85 Post-war model. Lorry SIS–150, Prototype taking part in the Sports Parade on the Red Square. Photo taken from the journal *USSR Under Construction,* 8, 1939.

86 Universal-1 tractor, serially produced at the Kirov Factory in Leningrad, 1934. – 87 Unknown designer: 'The Five Year Plan in Four Years', material pattern, 1930.

88

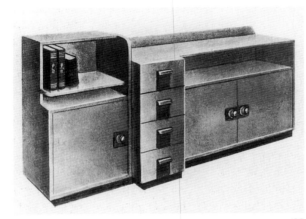

89

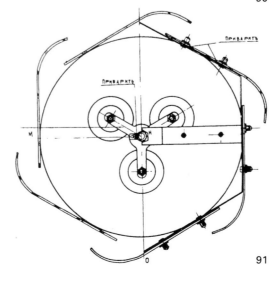

90

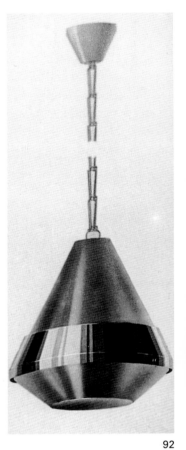

92

93

91

88 N Borov, G Samski, I Yang: design for a conference room in the *Pravda* Publishing House, Moscow, 1935. – 89 N Borov, G Samski, I Yang: office furniture for the editors of *Pravda,* 1932. – 90 and 91 Abram Damski: design for a lamp in the Pravda Building, 1932. – 92 Abram Damski: design for the *Lutsetta* overhead lamp, 1932. – 93 N Borov, G Samski, I Yang: chair for the cantine in the *Pravda* Building, 1932.

94

95

At this time design was also increasingly used as an ideological method to inform people and encourage them in the struggle. Porcelain, for example, depicted concrete images from the working world, Lenin portraits and declamatory exclamations ('Against exploitation' or 'If you don't work, you shouldn't eat') instead of earlier Constructivist patterns. Single objects such as presents for Stalin, public representative buildings for State and Party organs, large parks and exhibition halls and the way they were decorated, played a particular role in the increasing politicisation of almost all areas of applied art and architecture. Here thematic and formal considerations went hand in hand. On the other hand, some of the objects created by the new technology had an austere, classically cool look. Chandeliers were fitted with light-bulbs that looked like older lamps from below, demonstrating the return of traditional stylistic elements by reverting to older, but now anachronistic, artistic methods that appeared all the more alienated if their form stood in obvious contradiction to any form of functionality. One must remember, however, that the mass products of the thirties, with all their qualities, were not solely invented by engineers. Then, as before, artists and members of other professions were highly influential. Despite major changes in cultural policies, buildings were erected at the beginning of the thirties that had been planned a decade earlier. Their style was unmistakably influenced by Functionalism and Constructivism. The forms were composed of simple, geometric elements, with steel and concrete half-timbering and smooth, partially painted outer walls. An example of this is the

editorial and printing offices of *Pravda* in Moscow, constructed in 1934 according to designs by Ilia Golossov. The interior was built according to plans from the office of a group including, apart from Abram Damski, N Borov, G Samski and I Yang, amongst others. Damski had developed a number of rather original lamps at the VCHUTEMAS faculty of metalwork, amongst which was a globe made of frosted glass, hung from a mirror on a metal chain. Another similarly striking lamp consisted of six frosted glass leaves placed in a circular fashion, with edges that curl upwards. The stairways and halls of the *Pravda* building were lit by more decorative lamps, while Damski had designed functional lamps with moveable shades for the working spaces of editors, typesetters, sub-editors and printers.

A table lamp with metal shade by Damski, who worked for the General Electrotechnical Company at the time, continued being produced commercially, almost unchanged, until the sixties. Damski lamps, such as the ceiling lamp 'Lutsetta' (made of two cone-shaped parts), could be found in almost any house or institution. The more elegant version had metal edges, while the shade of the simpler version was usually made of frosted glass. In the following years, Damski designed lamps for the Moscow underground and skyscrapers, amongst others. Created at the beginning of the thirties, they reveal a completely different style. There are complicated constructions made of decorated glass parts (thrown into relief), cast aluminium or bronze, additionally decorated by diversely formed glitter-

96

97

98

99

ing additions. It was only in the fifties, alongside the overcoming of Stalinist art doctrines, that one returned to more simple lamp forms.

The interior decoration of the *Pravda* building's editorial and conference rooms, as well as of the working rooms and stairways, could be described as 'plastic Constructivism' (with some hesitation). Chairs, sofas, tables and shelves have carved droplet forms while the contours of the metal or wood frames of the chairs flow from the vertical to the horizontal and vice versa. A contribution to the publication *Architecture in the USSR* was positive about these although it appeared as if a new stylistic phase in furniture design was taking place. It also expressed doubts about what was considered force used by the Constructivists and what was considered the imitation of Western models. The steel-tube chairs after the Western European model were criticised. It was only in the chief editor's room that a 'return to older styles' was visible. The solution found for the interior decoration was, on the whole, satisfying. 'It must be noted that several areas looked back to former ideas and this regretably makes the brigade's work more difficult', even if they are 'talented enough to find noticeably independant and new solutions.'

Publications in the spirit of Constructivism and functional design were almost never published after 1934. Western European achievements in this area were criticised as being 'sterile' or 'inhuman'. And yet a more positive tone could be found in newspaper ar-

96 | Taranov: poster design for the Moscow Underground project 'The Best Transport in the Capital of the Proletariat', 1932. – 97 Nicolai Ladovsky: Dshershinskaya underground station in Moscow, Line 1, 1935. – 98 Escalator in a Moscow underground station. – 99 Clock with indicator for directions.

100

101

100 Initial design for the Krasno-
selskaya underground station in
Moscow, 1933. – 101 Vladimir
Stenberg: interior of the under-
ground compartments of the G
Series, late 1930s.

102

103

104

ticles about designs for the restructuring of the river promenade of the Moskva and the Communist University on the Vorobevy hills (later Moscow University). Curiously enough, these looked back to Michelangelo's stairway of the Biblioteca Laurentiana in Florence, as well as to the interiors of ancient palaces.

Undoubtedly a new style with as yet unforeseeable implications began to increasingly dampen any independent creativity. Maxim Gorki proclaimed the methods and aims of Socialist Realism for literature at the First Federal Literary Congress. These concepts soon influenced theatre, film and visual art and even changed the face of architecture with ingredients that in fact counteracted their aims. Interior decoration, book design, posters, newspapers and other printed matter, even decorating and clothing materials were examined for 'formalistic tendencies' and, if they failed to comply with the strict examination criteria, were branded as supposedly subversive ideas. Every exposed area could now become ideologically productive, whether through ornamentally reproduced motifs from technology with decorations using the Soviet star, ears of corn and oak leaves, or with images from life under Socialism, exuding joy. Porcelain and textile factories were often inspired by important technological achievments. The more banal the contents, the greater the aims of propaganda – 'Mechanisation of the RKKA' (Red Workers and Farmers Army), 'The Red Army at the Wool Harvest', 'The Fulfilment of the Five Year Plan in Four Years', 'The War Fleet'. Sport, the Red Army, aeronautics, industrialisation and ad-

102 Design for a Moscow underground station, 1930s. – 103 Train at a Moscow underground station, drawing, 1930s. – 104 12th Architectural Workshop of the Mossoviet: design for a *bureau de change,* 1934.

105 Ice-cream selling at an underground station. – 106 and 107 12th Architectural Workshop of the Mossoviet: design for a book kiosk in the underground, closed left, open right, 1934. – 108 12th Architectural Workshop of the Mossoviet: design for an underground bench, 1934.

105

106

107

vances in the reduction of illiteracy provided most of the subjects for film, photography, painting, sculpture and graphic art. Images of Lenin and Stalin were, however, of central importance. Several textile designs were used for agitative posters, complemented by appropriate pieces of text. Some possessed a certain degree of elegance, despite their ideological content, while others did not hide their debt to the geometric Constructivist tradition of the twenties and were forerunners of Op-art with their rapport between line and rectangle patterns. Many works of the new agitatory art were produced by students of the textile faculty of the VCHUTEMAS-VCHUTEIN. The composition course was headed by the painter Alexander Kuprin. A woman as important as Varvara Stepanova, Rodchenko's wife and co-worker taught at what was the best place for future textile designers to learn their trade as late as 1924–25. Her influence lasted until well into the thirties, despite arguments about anti-abstract art and so-called formalism.

108

109

Everyday Life

The contradiction between ideology and reality, between the needs and consumer behaviour of the population, on the one hand, and the Socialist vision of beauty proclaimed by State and Party, on the other, was reflected in the working and private life of any average Soviet citizen in the thirties. While he encountered products demonstrating technological progress in department stores, he also experienced the construction of monumental, representational buildings in which the same technology disappeared behind ecclectic elements, hidden by sculptures, mosaics and wall paintings of doubtful artistic merit. Their pathos was often stifling.

At least at the beginning of the thirties, formal design of everyday objects, interior decorative elements (above all of furniture), had a style combining usefulness and functionality with exterior compactness. Typical of this was the wide use of streamlined forms, found most often in the design of steel and aluminium pipes. The streamlined form, developed from the aerodynamic laws of lowest resistance, can be observed particularly well in the Moscow Mossoviet Hotel and several sanatoriums, as well as in the Maxim Gorki aeroplane and the OSGA-25 ship which has two hulls.

A committee was formed at the Architectural Academy in Moscow in 1935 to lay down formal rules for the design of everyday furniture, ironware, wooden handles, railings, locks and other objects. Illustrated books for factories

recommended certain designs. Most of the models were traditional. Metal objects were cast and wood was carved or sawed.

The inconsequential return to older forms pointed to the path a section of Russian design would follow. Conservatism also entered residential architecture. Model apartments built for the Party and State élite were filled with old-fashioned, voluminous furniture. The apartments themselves had rather traditional, comfortable dimensions with their hallways, lounges, bedrooms, dining rooms and guest rooms. The pleasant picture of everyday life in the Workers' and Peasants' State painted by the media stood in sharp contrast to the fact that the majority of the population lived in council housing where each family received one room at the most. Here it was a great advancement when gas-cookers replaced dangerous petroleum ovens, and central heating was introduced which was certainly welcomed although patience was needed. In a short while, hundreds of thousands of gas-cookers and gas water-heaters were needed, a demand that the GASOAPPARAT factory understandably failed to fulfil.

Life in council flats, today a subject highly favoured by film-makers, required the highest degree of sacrifice from those living in them. On the other hand, articles that had been unavailable for a long time, such as radios, came onto the market more frequently. Millions of these were manufactured in the Moscow Electrical Works and were linked to an extensive network. Listening to the acoustic pleasures provided by bands, classical music, news and

109 Streamlined steam locomotive 2-3-2, V-Series, manufactured in Kolomna, 1938. Photo: A Schaichet.

110

patriotic music made a lack of other comforts easier to bear.

Technological inventions were of central importance for many leisure and hobby clubs, as soon as large numbers of products appeared on the market. Periodicals for photography fans and amateur radio operators were highly popular. The amount of model aeroplane, car, radio and phono clubs rose annually. Cheap cameras were particularly in demand. The OGPU factory in Charkov manufactured the Soviet Leica FED in the early thirties. It was not only popular among reporters. A camera with mirror prisms, developed in the VOMP (Association for Optical and Mechanical Production) in 1935, was developed in a Leningrad factory in 1935 and was called 'Sport', as it was suitable for taking photos in stadiums. As was the case with a variation of this camera, the film could be reeled from one light-impervious cassette to another; the viewfinder was vertical although it could also be brought to a horizontal position.

111

112

There was enough laboratory equipment (sockets for developing, lamps, enlargement equipment, basins) available for professional photographers and amateurs, although it was a problem to set this up in a one-room apartment. Those who did not use their rooms as darkrooms at night built cupboards that could be folded or similar furniture of the kind the press always advocated people to construct themselves. Designing such pieces, according to precise instructions, followed the principle 'Need requires creativity' and made no artistic or aesthetic demands.

110 Electric suburban train, 1930. 111 Electric VL Series locomotive *(Vladimir Lenin),* manufactured from 1940 until the late 1950s. – 112 Streamlined steam locomotive 2-3-2, K-2 Series, manufactured in Kolomna, 1938–39.

Portable, clockwork-driven gramophones which could be taken on excursions in the countryside or on longer trips, attested to their owner's high standard of living but found relatively few buyers, despite advertisements in newspapers and periodicals. They embodied freedom of movement and joy and were also symbols of progress, emblems of a metropolitan lifestyle, enlivening the dullness of the everyday with spots of light.

The summer streets with ice-cream and mineral water sellers, snack-bars and cafés, as seen in many films of the time, are part of this rather light-hearted picture of Russian cities in the period before World War II. The designers received tasks which one can consider minor but which received the same public attention as posters, book covers or textile patterns. The right-angled booths of the lemonade vendors, with their trays and turntables for glasses and glass cylinders, could be found in Moscow until the late fifties. White, wooden stages, arbours and Neo-classical benches, as well as cement statues of young girls, also painted white, could be found in public parks. Booths, summer cafés with balustrades and sun-roofs, sports areas and smaller sports facilities invited people to take a rest.

These facilities, usually mobile and easy to dismantle, were often designed by relatively well known architects and designers. At the same time, one cannot overlook the fact that the professional status, sphere of activities and socially educational role of the designer in the thirties was not yet clearly defined. The designer led a shadowy existence alongside well known actors, writers, scientists, inventors and architects, even if he belonged to professional organisations along the lines of those created by artists.

Groups such as LEF (Left Art Front) or OKTIABR (October), created mainly by Constructivists in 1929, had not existed for those artists primarily concerned with design in the twenties. Several had joined the architectural association OSA, which had emerged from the Left Art Front in 1925. Even after this ceased to exist in 1932, the situation was unsatisfactory, becoming even more diffuse than before. It was only in large-scale projects with a clear assignment of tasks that the designer could compete equally with other participants (even surpassing them). The Five Year Plans (the first of which had replaced the free market

113

114

115

116

113 Conveyor belt in the Gorki (Nishni Novgorod) Car Factory with GAZ-A cars, 1932. Photo: E Langman. – 114 Racing car, developed from the GAZ-A model. Still from the film *At the Steering-Wheel* by Lev Kuleshov, 1928. – 115 Valentin Brodski: KIM-1 car (KIM is short for 'Communist International of Youth'), 1940.

116 Vladimir Meshtsherin: Lorry of the SIS-Series, 1938. – 117 Lorry of the SIS-5 type, 1930s. At the left in the background is the lightweight lorry GAZ-AA, manufactured in Gorki (Nishni Novgorod).

117

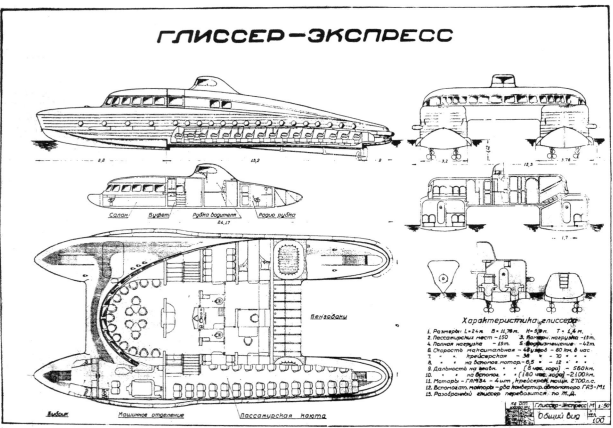

ГЛИССЕР—ЭКСПРЕСС

Салон Буфет Рубка водителя Радио рубка
24,17

Бензобаки

Выборка Машинное отделение Пассажирская каюта

Характеристика глиссера

1. Размеры: L=24м B=11,78м H=5,9м T=1,4м.
2. Пассажирских мест –150 3. Полезн. нагрузка –13т.
4. Полная нагрузка –19т. 5. Водоизмещение –42т.
6. Скорость максимальная – 48 узлов – 80 км. в час
7. " крейсерская – 38 " – 70 "
8. " на вспомог. мотор– 6,5 " – 12 "
9. Дальность на главн. " [8 час. хода] – 560км.
10. " на вспомог. " [180 час. хода] –2100км.
11. Моторы – ГАМ34 – 4 шт. крейсерск. мощн. 2700л.с.
12. Вспомогат. моторы –два конвертир. автомотора ГАЗ-М1
13. Разобранный глиссер перевозится по ж.д.

Глиссер-Экспресс М 1:50
Общий вид 100

119

118 Vladimir Meshtsherin: the hovercraft catamaran OSGA-25, drawing, 1936–37. – 119 Vladimir Meshtsherin: construction drawing for the OSGA-25 hovercraft catamaran, 1937. V Gartwig was chief project designer.

120

121

122

123

strategies of the New Economic Policy in 1928) meant that there was no lack of these in the thirties. Huge industrial projects, the construction of the Moscow underground, urban planning that affected old city structures, the construction of new residential areas and whole cities, alongside Soviet industrial developments, made the masses loyal to the State, willing to make sacrifices, work in collectives and take pride in any technological development. At the same time, the freedom to create individual lifestyles decreased. The chances for architects and designers to influence the technical and cultural development of the Soviet Union with ideas departing from official cultural policies also decreased. The danger of being suspected of 'formalism' was always imminent.

Foreign attitudes to this situation were ambivalent. The exhibition the Soviet Union brought to various large American cities in 1929, showing industrial and craft artefacts, was as successful as the participation in the *Exposition internationale des arts décoratifs et industriels modernes* in Paris four years earlier. A lack of artistic experimentation could be observed in exhibitions in Western Europe and the USA – it had still been present at the PRESSA in Cologne (1928) and in travelling shows of Soviet art in Vienna, London, Berlin and Stockholm in 1930. A certain uniformity was prevalent, excluding technological exhibits. Therefore mosaics, paintings, coloured glass windows, scupltures and ceramic artefacts with good formal qualities that did not depict the usual State emblems or subjects such as Red Army members, workers and

120 Model of the hovercraft catamaran OSGA-25, 1937. – 121 Vladimir Meshtsherin: chair for the first class on the bridge between the hulls of the catamaran OSGA-25, drawing, 1936–37. – 122 Vladimir Meshtsherin: seats for the second class in the interior of the OSGA-25 ship, drawing, 1936–37. – 123 The construction of the OSGA-25 catamaran, 1937–38.

124

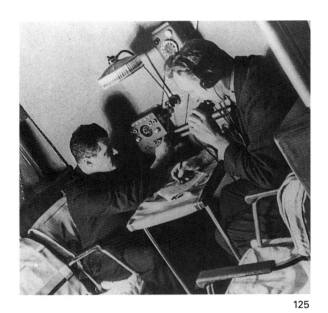

125

peasants, stood out all the more. The trend towards formal uniformity, with only minor variability even in design details, naturally developed most strongly where there was least competition. The masses did not, for the most part, take note of this or only to the degree in which production allowed for comparison and choice. This was not, however, the case in certain sectors of the textile industry. Here, above all, with working and sports clothes, efficiency was more important than fashionable and individual forms of taste. Sport and 'Spartacus' parades (with the motto 'Ready for Work and Defence') had a great influence on young people's clothing. White shirts and canvas shoes, belonging to such gatherings, were amongst the most popular items of youth fashion in the thirties.

126

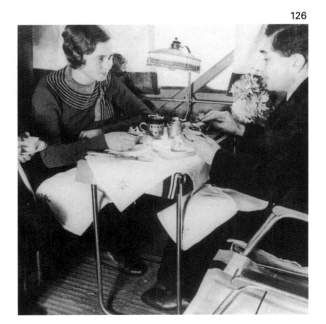

124 Cockpit of the *Maxim Gorki* aeroplane, 1935. – 125 Radio operator's cabin on board the *Maxim Gorki,* 1935. – 126 A meal in the passenger cabin of the *Maxim Gorki,* 1935.

127 The *Maxim Gorki,* archive picture with the stamp 'TSAGY. Reproduction prohibited.'
128 Cabins in the *Maxim Gorki.* From the periodical *The Building Up of the Soviet Union,* 1, 1935.

127

128

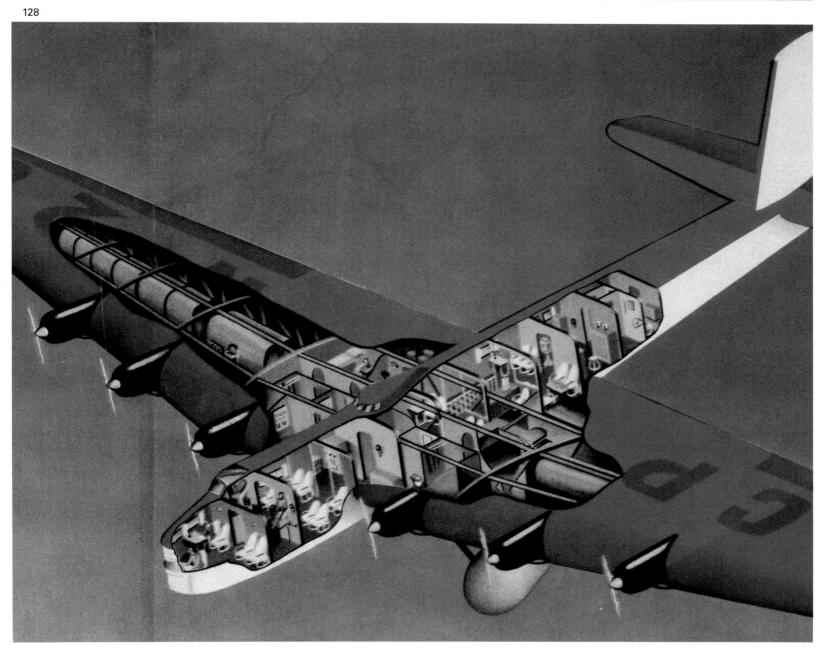

129

131

132

133

130

Large Public Projects

Many of the competition designs handed in for the State Theatre in Charkov and the Moscow Soviet Palace originated from American and Western European architectural offices. The chances of realisation for these projects was minor from the onset. It is more important to stress the fact that architectural competitions with international participants were actually held at this period of Soviet cultural politics. The exhibition showing work from the last twenty years of the Bauhaus Dessau (opened in the summer of 1931 in Moscow), the centre of progressive form and architecture, is of particular significance in the light of subsequent developments. Some years later, after the decree to reorganise artistic life in line with Socialist Realism as the sole art form of the USSR (1934), cultural self-isolation had reached high levels. 'Counter-revolutionary' tendencies were rigorously fought against, in the cinema, literature and in other areas of art with similar fixations on the Soviet citizen working heroically for the fulfilment of the Five Year Plan, brimming with Socialist ideas and believing in a joyful future. The working day, however, was more sober than when seen in films or on posters. Although the

129 Vladimir Tatlin: *Letatlin* flying machine, 1929–32. Reconstructed from original parts 1960–70, State Museum for Air Travel and Aeronautics, Monino. – 130 *Letatlin* at the Federal Inventor's Exhibition at the Polytechnic Museum in Moscow, 1937. Photo: A Rodchenko.

131–133, 135–137 Stills from the film *Flight to the Moon,* Mosfilm, 1935.

134

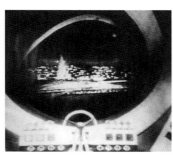

135

136

137

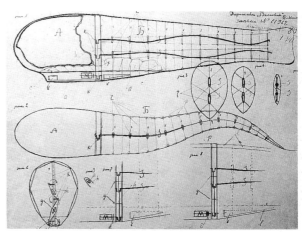

138

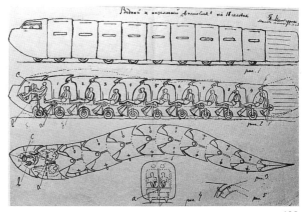

139

wages of industrial workers had been reduced and lean economic times continued, the transformation of the Soviet Union into a highly technical state was taking place (with the construction of dams, canals, factories and highways). The Moscow underground is one of the first great achievements attesting to this progress. It changed the face of the city in the thirties (today with a population of eleven million), not least through the work of countless designers. A graphic artist, Lazar Rappaport, created the first logo with his strong, stylised 'M'. Drivers, ticket collectors and other personnel, including train station ice-cream vendors, received their own uniforms. Collectives with well known architects like Alexander Dushkin, Ivan Fomin, Nikolai Kolli and Dmitri Chechulin gave each underground station an unmistakable face, with additions by painters and sculptors. Initial designs by I Taranov (1931) already displayed the linking of the planned lines with important urban points, as well as escalators, the placement of the platforms, entrances and exits.

When the first line was opened in 1935 (the second, three years later), a dream of the future was fulfilled. In the twenties, it had not only been traffic experts who believed that the

134 Airship models (with neon lighting) at the Federal Inventors Exhibition at the Polytechnic Museum in Moscow, 1937. – 138 and 139 Piotr Miturich: projects for an airship with snake-like hull, and for a 'caterpillar car', made of single parts, drawings for the application for a patent, 1931.

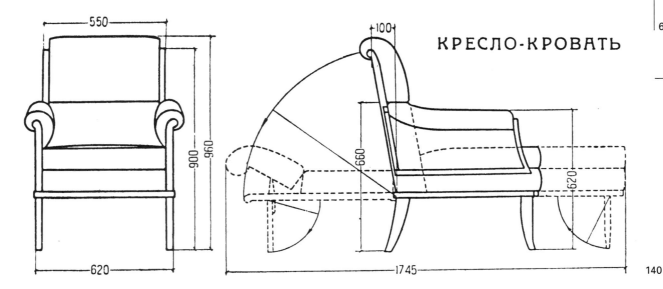

КРЕСЛО-КРОВАТЬ

140

141

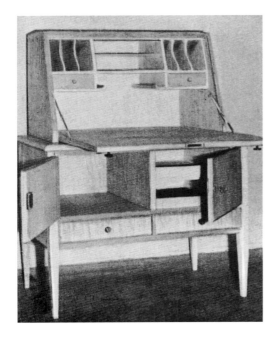

142

chaos and overcrowding of the Moscow streets would cease with the advent of an underground. In 1932 it was worked out that each tram waggon in Moscow had a yearly average of 90,000 passengers. This was another reason for speeding up the underground project as fast as possible. P Lopatin stated that without an underground 'one would not be able to live in Moscow in the future'. In his book he describes the underground platforms with trains stopping every one-and-a-half minutes, stands for newspapers, cigarettes and drinks, precise movements of travel controllers and tiny lights marking out the network – a self-sufficient world, including pay counters, turnstiles, benches and advertising areas boards. They were designed by a group of designers who had partaken in the design of the *Pravda* building's interior.

'Aerodynamic' forms, typical of the design of transportation in the thirties, characterised the exterior of many stands and cashdesks. Lightly vaulted, flowing areas and gleaming metal details gave the impression of well-run functionality in a technically highly developed system. All details were linked like clockwork. Particular emphasis was placed on visual information, helping to indicate stations for changing trains, network plans and easily legible signs. The design of several underground stations obviously influenced construction projects taking place at the same time. It was itself also inspired by ideas from older architectural styles (such as Neo-classicism). This applies, for example, to the Dsherdashinskaia station, after designs by Nikolai Ladovski, a former VCHUTEMAS professor.

140 Design for a chair which can be converted into a bed. It was manufactured by the Union of Woodwork Cooperatives in the 1930s. – 141 and 142 Chest of drawers, combined with a desk; closed (above) and open (below), 1930s.

143

144

145

146

143 Design studio of the Mossoviet Hotel: chair for the Hotel Moscow 1933. – 144 E Gushinskaya: chair for a sanatorium, 1934. – 145 L Saveliev, O Stapran: lounge in one of the two-room appartments in the Mossoviet Hotel Moscow 1933. – 146 Design studio of the Mossoviet Hotel: bedside table, 1933. – 147 E Gushinskaya: bed for a sanatorium, 1934.

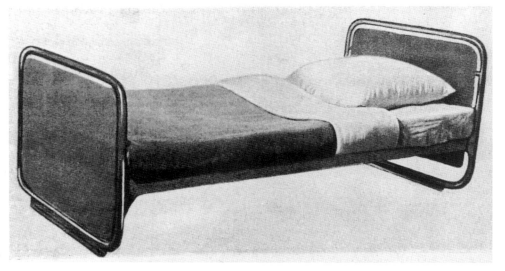

147

148

149

The majority of stations opened in 1938, however, demonstrated what was a more or less smooth transition to the new, monumental 'palace style' which included a great deal of sculpture and mosaics. The Berlin underground provided inspiration for the compartments but instead of the three-door compartment (type A), however, there were four doors. The seats and wall divisions were also modified. The lamps for this first series of compartments, designed by Dimitri Saonegin, appeared like comfortable wall lighting and came from the ELECTROSVET factory in Moscow.

Vladimir Sternberg, co-founder of the Association of Young Artists (OBMOCHU) in 1919 – later responsible for the decoration of the Red Palace during festivities – participated in the design of the underground before the onset of World War II. The most striking novelties were soft, leather seats, drop-like lamps and the amalgamation of the seats into compartments instead of the usual formation, parallel to the windows. Several of these were constructed and used during the War although later the division between the compartments fell into disfavour. Only the style of the rails, lamps, doors, window and wall designs were maintained until the seventies.

Recent attempts to bring about modernisation of old-fashioned underground lighting, replacing bulbs with lighter halogen lamps without changing the (now almost historical) lamp forms, met with difficulties. A reasonably satisfying solution does not appear to be in sight. Even if modifications were to take place, nothing would change the museum character of the underground, with its strange mixture of the most diverse forms and stylistic elements combined with what was considered exemplary technology. Formerly celebrated and now integrated into everyday life, today the Moscow underground is a method of transport like any other. Only the older generation looks back at it nostalgically (before the onset of a new century) with a feeling similar to that of air travel veterans looking at out-moded planes.

In the thirties, the Soviet Union made great advances in aeoronautics in order to keep up with international developments. This was also in its own interests, due to the great expanses of land which were still unreachable by any means of transport. Additionally, hope was placed on propagandistic effects. Most

148 Telephone booth in the shape of a telephone, 1930s. – 149 Metal telephone booth, prototype, 1932.

150

151

150 Café furniture made of wicker, 1930s. – 151 Street booth for selling fruit and vegetables, 1932. – 152 Open terrace of the Café Summer in Moscow, 1935. Photo: N Kuleshov.

152

important, however, was the technically innovative spirit of the designers, enriched symbiotically by the creativity of enthusiastic creators of form. Without enough funding or optimal public support, however, even highly original projects, such as the agitative Maxim Gorki aeroplane, were bound to fail.

In 1934, many newspapers published an appeal by Russian writers making a plea for donations to set up an agitatory flying squadron. Donors were asked to make payments to a special account. The results of this and other similar advertisements was significant. Tupolev thus designed a variation of the ANT-20 transport aeroplane. The hull and wings were made of corrugated aluminium which allowed for barely any curves, so that the machine appeared more like a ship than an aeroplane. Two additional Mikrojan propeller mechanisms had been added in order to enlarge the load-bearing capacity. The telephones came from the Krasnaia Zaria Factory in Leningrad, a station for 16 connections. Due to the engine noise, there was no ringing. Instead, small lights lit up.

The radio factory in Gorki built the radio station for medium and long waves (reaching up to 2000 kilometres) while the surprisingly light generators were developed in the Electrosila Factory in Moscow to supply power to machines and other appliances. The commander could also contact his radio operators by pneumatic dispatch system. A projection room with screens of 4.5 x 6 metres, a snackbar, washrooms with showers and toilets, and later even a small printing machine (especially constructed for this plane), light metal chairs and tablecloths after designs by the former VCHUTEIN textile faculty – all made the Maxim Gorki the epitomy of technically perfected air-travel comfort, without comparable examples anywhere else.

Public reactions were appropriately enthusiastic. The special issue about the wonderful machine issued by the periodical *The Building Up of the USSR* was in the form of a separate brochure, all in silver, by the photographic artist, V Troshin. Each of the delegates in the Peoples Congress received a copy as a gift. Therefore, there was great sorrow when the Maxim Gorki crashed during an air show in 1936 (there was only one machine of this type) with all the crew and several passengers killed.

153

154

153 *Dukat* cigarette packaging, 1930s. Photo: P Kleptikov. – 154 Confectionary display, 1930s.

155

156

The express hydroplane OSGA-25 was fit for use and lasted over a longer period of time. A department for the development of hydroplanes and air-ships had already been formed in the twenties at AVTODOR, a voluntary group for the development of automobile and street traffic. The prototypes for the ships that were to be used on the Moskva and Volga passenger lines were developed here. Later, in the mid-thirties, it attempted to develop a large hydroplane of the catamaran type under the leadership of the chief designer, V Gartwig. Vladimir Meshtsherin, a VCHUTEIN graduate, designed a salon with chairs and lamps, a ticket booth, souvenirs and other items for this aircraft. The metal frame of the chairs consisted of tubes linked to one another and could be swung upwards to surround the seating area, giving an impression of security. The contours of the furniture, windows and details such as hooks or handles blended in with the streamlined form of the ship. Some of the furnishings consisted of synthetic materials (which were being used to an increasingly great extent) – the possibilities for using this sculpturally were exploited completely.

Twenty-four metres long and twelve metres wide, the OSGA-25 had remarkable measurements, without appearing heavy. The observa-tion room in the front of the craft, between the hulls of the catamaran, as well as the bridge, appeared to consist of a single part. The hydroplane, which could accommodate 150 people and achieve a velocity of 80 km per hour, was used for the Yalta-Sevastopol route in 1938, after several years of construction. With four express and two reserve engines, the comfortable functionality and modernity of the interior and the aerodynamic form, enabling the boat to glide over the waves like a flying object over the waves, embodied the highest technical standards, possibly the reason why it could not be photographed. During the war, when German troops threatened Odessa with occupation, orders were given to destroy the OSGA-25 (so that it would not fall into enemy hands). The engines were removed and the hull was cut apart – the whereabouts of these pieces have never been ascertained.

The economic usefulness of inventions (limited to being unique examples of technology) had little power to gain prestige for State and Party leadership. One the other hand, there was a certain agreement between the people's naive belief in progress and the constantly repeated slogans asking for ever greater achievements for the development and growth of Socialism. It is therefore no wonder that the picture of the future, inspiring the

155 Porcelain tableware in a display window, 1930s. Photo: A Skuritshin. – 156 Design for a gas stove, 1935–37.

157

158

159

masses to constantly achieve more, was romantically rosy, if not utopian. Poets and composers who were faithful to the Party contributed to this. The text to the *Air March* proclaimed that 'we are born so that fairy-tales are turned to fact'. Or: 'We were given the ability to reason. Instead of arms, we received wings and instead of a heart, an engine'. Technological progress was presented as the logical result of social processes and every actual improvement was seen as proof of social perfection.

The idea of two interdependent processes could be particularly well demonstrated by the possibilities of photography. Press photos, photo collages, film sequences, enlargements made into posters and diagrams: each shot could present a manilpulated view of reality and banality could be transformed into something fascinatingly new by changing perspectives, double exposure, sharp constrasting light and other effects. It was difficult to remain immune to these pictures for long. They appeared in social reports, for example, which described humiliating work, hunger and repression under the Kulaks (farmers with middle to large farms who had been forced into belonging to collectives). On the other hand, pictures of beaming faces, joyful about the first Five Year Plan, had a visual pathos that allowed little room for doubt or at least mitigated it.

The young avant-garde's enthusiasm, eagerness to experiment and undaunted belief in technology appeared to continue (where it had not become stultified into formulary agi-

157 First Russian television. The picture is transmitted by mirror reflector, the tone via radio, 1930s. – 158 *Sport* mirror reflex camera for 135 mm film, 1936. – 159 A record from the 1930s.

160

tation) and they developed utopian, visionary ideas. This can be found in poster art of the early thirties. In an exhibition at the Polytechnical Museum in Moscow one could find the most diverse objects: Tatlin's aeroplane covered in material and reminiscent of a dove, as well as lathes above which were recommendations about rationalising labour. Models of aeroplanes that had already been constructed or were in the planning stages hung in another room, dedicated to air travel. Further designs revealed completely new methods of transport. A large diagram showed the streamlined forms of the engineer Waldner's one-track railway that sped along a high track. The compartments of the train, given power by propellers, gripped the tracks from two sides. Even more exotic was the project by the artist, Piotr Miturich – this construction was to move both in air and water by means of complicated mechanisms that had the appearance of a fish's tail.

In these years of burgeoning technological, experimental fantasies and visions of the future, the film *Flight to the Moon* was made, a gold-mine for film architects and designers. The Kim Voroshilov rocket of the Narkom Oborony (Peoples Commissioner for Defence) was launched from a pad in the centre of Moscow. On its flight the crew left a non-existant capital behind: the screen on which Earth was observed revealed a huge Soviet palace with a 100 metre high statue of Lenin on the roof, a symbol of the fulfilment of dreams that could be seen from afar and was becoming more and more possible. As late as 1937, a completely new centre for Moscow had been

based on the competition designs of Boris Iofan (1931–32). This included a palace with a large base to accommodate an oversized statue of Lenin.

Plans designed to overcome concrete, everyday problems (such as the modernisation and expansion of traffic over long and short distances) which aimed at a visible improvement of general living standards were naturally easier to realise than huge projects with obviously irrational traits. The Scientific Institute for Urban Transport (NIIGT) and the Institute for Automobiles and Automotors (NAMI-A) developed new types of buses and trams that were more modern and spacious than before. The streamlined SIS-16 bus, based on a new lorry model, was built in 1938. Streamlined forms, having become more and more popular, also characterised the exterior of the steam engine of the IS series and the railcar that travelled between Moscow and Leningrad. There were, however, tendencies that took a different course. This was usually in the form of details, such as the steam engines of the K-1 series whose tank wagon sides carried the gold coat of arms of the USSR and the five-point star with Stalin's portrait sculpted in the middle.

It was obvious that modern, streamlined forms were not favoured by conservative designers, much less by State and Party functionaries, concerned with educating the masses. They were despised as attributes of a bourgeois, Western lifestyle and a government resolution even tried to ban them although this had little success. It was indeed

161

more than just a 'bourgeois' fashion, as it was labelled. In the early twenties A Nikitin, a junior civil servant of one of the military academies, had undertaken initial, pioneering experiments by placing a steamlined bodywork on the frame of the GAZ-A automobile. What was a highly stylish car profile at the time is clearly recognisable in a film made at a car race in 1928. The ideologically based resistance to aerodynamic forms was forsaken, partly because it had succeeded in air travel in 1933-34, after a long period of development. At that time hope was placed in air travel as an example of technological progress and an experimental field for gifted engineers to constantly make new discoveries (Andrei Tupolev being the most important). Moreover, the fact that streamlined forms had new possibilities for technology and design – useful for products in many industrial branches – could not be overlooked. Instead of constructing frames, designers concentrated more on the design of covers and surfaces (for example, in car factories on designs of bodywork, headlamps, coolers and so on).

The Soviet automobile industry had been influenced by foreign products for too long. Almost all cars produced in the second half of the thirties were still modifications of Western models (for example the GAZ-A and M-1 Emka variations of the Ford). The realisation of its own potential took place only shortly before World War II with the construction of the SIS lorry. The periodical *The Building Up of the USSR* depicted one of these with its white cabins on the Red Square in Moscow at one of the usual sports parades. The first small Soviet car, called KIM (International Communist Youth), was presented shortly after war broke out. It had streamlined bodywork but also a running board that could be lowered, created by the designer, Valentin Brodski.

The invasion of the Soviet Union by Hitler's Germany made a great impact on the economic situation and on all other aspects of life. Changing production in favour of the arms industry forced many other areas into retreat. Defending the country took precedence over the construction of palaces of culture or the development of new furniture and lamps. The World Exhibitions in Paris (1937) and New York (1939) had given the country what was to be a last chance to show the state of Soviet crafts and industrial culture (with selected examples) for a long time. In the Soviet Union itself, it was the Federal Farming Exhibition in 1940 in Leningrad that demanded a high level of design, both in exhibits and exterior design,

162

161 Liubov Popova: *Industrial* tea set, c 1930, manufactured by the State Porcelain Factory in Leningrad. – 162 Mitrofan Rukavishnikov: *Boderguard* table lamp, 1934.

163

and was the last large show of this kind before the interval enforced by the war.

Several designers of the first two generations had emigrated abroad. Gustav Klutsis, former member of INCHUK and one of the most important designers of posters, was arrested in 1938, after having taken part in the Paris World Exhibition in the previous year, and died during deportation. Alexei Gan, a poster artist and designer also known outside the Soviet Union, had emerged as one of the most radical Contructivists in the twenties but died in 1940, a year before Nikolai Ladovski and El Lissitsky, the most multi-faceted and influential veterans of the avant-garde (alongside Tatlin and Rodchenko). Rodchenko himself worked on various photo reports until 1941, after which he created agitatory posters and exhibits for a state information bureau. Other designers survived as photo journalists, members of publishing houses, teachers at art and architectural institutes or as film and theatre designers, as long as they were not officially banned from working and exibiting. Still others were victims of the war, such as those that fell during the Siege of Leningrad.

164

163 Liya Raitser: material design 'Mechanisation of the Red Army', 1933. – 164 Design office Andrei Tupolev: military transport aeroplane, 1935.

165

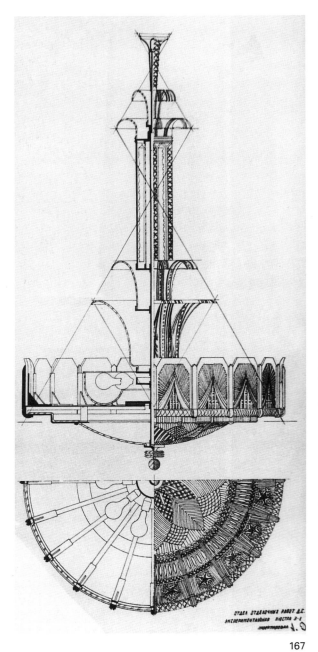

167

166

165 *Sea Fleet,* material design, early 1930s. – 166 Abram Damski: design for an overhead lamp for the Palace of the Soviets in Moscow, 1938. – 167 *Joseph Stalin* steamboat, 1938.

168

169

168 Limousine from the Joseph Stalin Carworks in Moscow, 1930s. Photo: M Prechner.
169 Urydova: Kreml-shaped perfume flask, 1930s.

3 NEW BEGINNINGS

171

New Beginnings

A design does not necessarily have to be new although it can help to break through routine and sluggish ways of seeing.
G Botsharov

After World War II a great deal of creative energy was set free after the reopening of the art and design schools that had been partially or completely closed. Soviet art, however, was not freed of the State and Party domination. The group fighting against 'formalistic' ideas or tendencies, appearing dangerous for the class struggle, had become even stronger, compared to the pre-war years. The consequences were terrible and, at times, grotesque. Books, usually decorated by laurel and oak leaves on the outside, often had a portrait of Stalin on the cover (in the forties and fifties) even if their subject matter was completely different from the achievements of the great man who believed himself to be the sole authority on all areas, including culture. At the end of the forties, the Central Committee of the Soviet Communist Party passed a resolution to combat so-called cosmopolitanism. This instructed all Soviet artists to fight Western influences (appealing to patriotism whilst warning the masses at the same time).

The highly necessary completion of practical tasks, the repair of war damage, the rebuilding of cities and destroyed industries was not affected by such regimentation. Ideology and building bridges did not complement one another although new street or river crossings were given fine-sounding names after heroes of the Workers' Movement, the Party or the Great War of the Fatherland. The situation in the initial post-war years demanded a high degree of improvisation, as well as training and a willingness to work collectively, from designers. The successors of the old Stroganov School, the VCHUTEMAS-VCHUTEIN, were reopened in 1945 (as was the Leningrad counterpart). Sachar Bykov, a former pupil of Alexander Rodchenko, became Rector of the Higher Industrial College in Moscow. While design students prepared themselves for future tasks, offices were created that were not simply linked to a factory, working solely for this, but which carried out contracts for various companies. The ACHB (Architectural Art Office), headed by Yuri Soloviev, achieved a certain amount of autonomy. Designs for a trolley bus, the interior of a vacation steamer and the cabins of the ice-breaking Lenin machine (fuelled by atomic energy) were created at the ACHB during the fifties. Soloviev also took up the idea of multi-purpose furniture again.

In the first years he was faced with the difficulty of discovering new talents who were artistically gifted with a keen sense of style, who had technical and construction abilities and also had a knowledge gained from practical training, if possible. The second problem was attempting to successfully explain to industrial leaders what design is, what it aims to achieve and how it can benefit society, both aesthetically and materially. Soloviev com-

170 Design office Andrei Tupolev: passenger aeroplane type TU-104, 1957.

171 Type MTB-82M omnibus, produced in the Tushino Factory since 1946. Type GAZ-20 *Pobeda* car, after a design by W Samoilov, manufactured since 1946 in the Gorki (Nishni Novgorod) Car Factory. Photo: G Petrusov.

172

173

174

172 Type GAZ-20 *Pobeda* car, engraving. – 173 Type SIS-110 limousines in the factory, in rows, ready for inspection, 1949. Photo: I Shagin. – 174 Type SIS-110 limousine as an ambulance, manufactured 1945–51 in the Joseph Stalin Carworks in Moscow.

175

176

pleted his educational work 'from above' by attempting to convince leading industrial workers of the advantages of functional forms (showing superbly designed products). Good design was not created by intuition and artistic experience alone, but also by knowing and using scientific knowledge (from anthropometry and ergonomics, for example). Additionally, it was important to have technological knowledge, experience of previous modes of production and the courage to modify them, if necessary.

At the beginning of his career, Soloviev created designs for renewing the compartments of the State Railway. The Ministry for Transport Construction had contracted to the Railway Compartment Factory in Kalinin (Tver) to develop a compartment combining maximum comfort with costs that were as low as possible. Soloviev, asked for help and advice by the factory's construction office, collected together a working group of several designers. The results were impressive under the circumstances of the time, and could be compared to a model designed by other engineers.

The difference between the competing designs and the compartments of the older type was enormous. The latter housed narrow windows, small, uncomfortable seats and dull lighting, while the two new designs embraced interiors which were both generous and functional, with curved edges and corners. The design by Soloviev and his co-workers J Somova, G Lebedev and I Kulakov was superior to that presented by the engineers, due to the

175 Type GAZ-12 ZIM limousine as an ambulance, manufactured 1949–1959 by the Molotov Carworks. – 176 Working on the type SIS-154 diesel bus in the Joseph Stalin Carworks in Moscow, 1947. Photo: I Shagin.

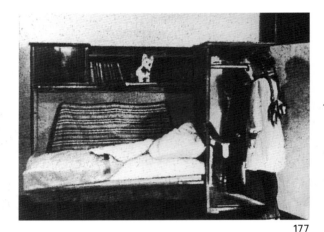

177

178

179

quality of detail, space-saving, moveable seats, folding tables in the corridors and other practical elements that took the traveller's needs into account (for example, aluminium ashtrays on the armrests). The compartments are still produced today, after approximately half-a-century, without any great changes in design. Soloviev's success meant that his office was adjoined to a department of the Ministry for Transport Construction in 1946.

When the state organisation for the entire Soviet civil aviation, Aeroflot, widened its flight network inland and abroad in the fifties, it received a new 'outfit'. Architects, engineers and designers from diverse backgrounds came together to create new waiting-rooms, install information boards and mobile gangways and design a new emblem. Modernity was limited to the exterior of the new machines, jet aircrafts of the TU-104 type. The interiors, however, had a rather old-fashioned charm, much like the luxury compartments of express trains with blankets and curtains with crochet patterns, comfortable table lamps and other 'Russian style' elements. Attempts at functionality were hidden under rather contrived decorative details, now and then with a folkloric flavour.

All this contrasted with the contact with international design. This was the case during the Khruschev era, if not before. Primary steps towards this had already been taken by the automobile industry in the late forties. A new

bus with rounded bodywork, developed in the first post-war years, was still modelled on a pre-war type. Designers such as Y Dolmatovski, V Rostkov and V Ariamov, however, managed to liberate themselves from previous ideas. They regarded the automobile – at least its exterior – as an object that could be designed in many ways, flexibly, according to the position of the engine, the axes and the supports for seats and loading area. Engineering techniques and new demands on mobility and dynamics were combined with designing a form that also took aerodynamic and aesthetic elements into account. The small cars Sputnik and Belka are examples.

Technological developments in other fields, such as ship building, were presented to the people with great propaganda and were celebrated by the press. Industrial production was still linked to successful, Socialist progress and competition with Capitalism. Projects attempting to outdo the technological standard of Western products were supported greatly by the State, whereas manufacturing ordinary products were given sub-standard attention. Moreover, the unwieldiness of the bureaucratic apparatus, the arbitrariness of ministerial decisions and the inflexibility that was a deliberate part of the planned economy delayed the realisation of several truly progressive ideas.

At the same time, technicians and designers had successes again and again. A working

177 and 178 Yuri Soloviev, Svetlana Loginova: multi-purpose furniture for a child's room (cupboard, bed, table), 1947. – 179 Yuri Soloviev, J Somov, with G Lebedev and I Kulakov as coworkers: interior of a train compartment, 1946.

180

181

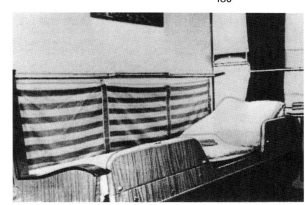

182

183

180 and 181 Yuri Soloviev with T Shepeleva: type SIU-5 omnibus, driver's cabin and overall view, designed in 1946, prototype built in 1955, produced serially since 1959. – 182 and 183 Svetlana Loginova: cabin of the *Lenin* icebreaker which used atomic power, 1957.

group was formed in 1958 in Gorki (renamed Nishni Novgorod) that was to design speedboats in the following years. Graduates of the Industrial Art School in Leningrad belonged to this group (F Pribyshtshenko, O Frolov, V Kvasov, A Frolov, I Medvedev and B Boikin) which is now the St Petersburg Industrial Art Institute. They developed the capabilities of the winged boats of the Meteor, Vichr and Comet series (created solely with functional aspects in mind) although their speed was less than that of the gas turbine boats from the Burevestnik series (97 kilometres per hour). In this case, the elegant form counted more.

The 1968 Soviet Exhibition in Warsaw had a highly modern aesthetic, with examples from transportation and heavy-duty industry. Amongst the most spectacular exhibits were the air-cushion ship from the Krasnoie Sormovo factory, developed for passenger travel; and the supersonic TU-144 aeroplane. It is revealing that the Federal Scientific Research Institute (VNIITE) took part in preparing the exhibition. The organisers wanted to show technological feats, appropriate for the state of the industries represented in Warsaw and present the 'packaging' of the exhibits well. These were hardly less impressive than their contents. During the Cold War, with threats from all sides, Soviet designers were often suspected of imitating Western design ideas. Stalin's death (1953) did not put a stop to the cultural doctrines he had created. Russian avant-garde art in the museums from the time before the Revolution and from the twenties remained under lock and key. Architecture was still dominated by the highly monotonous, pseudo-

184

185

186

Classical, monumental style that almost made Tatlin's Monument for the Third International appear prehistoric. For many, the Fifth World Festival of Youth and Students, held in Moscow in 1957, was the first opportunity, after long isolation, for establishing contact with people from other nationalities, fashions and ideas. There was a new feeling in the air, more cosmopolitan and critical, with a more differentiated attitude towards contemporary problems, mistrustful of the cult figures of the most recent period of Soviet history and the Party's unconditional demand for leadership.

In 1962, the Ministerial Council of the USSR passed a resolution advocating the founding of design offices to create machines and everyday objects. Industrial design, including furniture and textile design, was therefore a part of State production. In the years before this, articles in books, periodicals and newspapers addressing trends in popular culture painted a highly contradictory picture. Progressive ideas were, even if falteringly, connected to the pioneering work of Rodchenko, Tatlin, Lissitsky, Stepanova and Popova and could be found in conservative publications

184 Yuri Dolmatovski, Vladimir Ariamov and others: type NAMI-013 limousine, model, 1950–53. – 185 and 186 Yuri Dolmatovski, Vladimir Ariamov and others: town and country versions of the small *Belka* car (type IMS-NAMI-A50). The town car has a front and back flap, the country version has a removeable flap.

187

188

187 *Tsheka* limousine for seven passengers, manufactured at the Gorki (Nishni Novgorod) Car Factory, 1960s. – 188 Mosgorsovnakhos Design Office with A Gulzev: parliamentary limousine, model for the SIL Factory in Moscow, 1962–63.

189

such as *The Construction of a Residential Building,* published by the Architectural Academy in 1954. One could hardly accuse the authors of taking into account an optimal use of space or thinking how the mass need for furniture and other objects used in the home could be satisfied. Pictures revealed rooms with highly modest furnishings. On closer inspection, however, one saw that this interior decoration was suitable only for a four- or five-room apartment, with light rooms that had ledges, stucco ceilings, built-in cupboards and sliding doors. Athough appearing to be for large segments of the population at first glance, this was, in fact, advice for the privileged, for wealthy families and members of the nomenclatura. It was therefore appropriate that pieces had Chippendale or Sheraton elements, above all in the types of ornamantal moulding, painting and varnishing. Although furniture factories had made noteworthy achievements in previous years, 'the exaggerated proportions of the furniture and high prices prevented their use in the apartments of ordinary people.' Therefore, it was advised: 'it is better to have less furniture than a prettier interior and better to make use of the whole room with practical furniture.'

The demand for such furniture grew in proportion to the attempts made by the apartment building programme in the sixties. The concrete apartment blocks erected at the time needed a completely new type of furniture. The massive, bulky, heavy, pre-war furniture took up most of the limited space in the rooms; and it was necessary to develop lighter furniture. Designers did, in fact, reveal a space-saving profile – table and chair legs, standing lamps and chairs grew narrower towards the bottom. At the same time, however, so-called 'montage furniture,' made from clipboard emerged. Due to unwieldy dimensions and great weight, assembling it almost demanded a basic knowledge of architecture. Their system corresponded exactly with the way the houses in which they stood were constructed. Prefabricated, standardised parts were added to each other. Decorations on the front of bookshelves and cupboards with varying patterns, designed by artists or taken from historical examples, attempted to give an impression of a certain amount of cosiness and to reinforce old, bourgeois ideals of living. This was a great contradiction that had roots in the design itself, obviously lacking the courage to give up decorative elements completely.

189 Area in front of the 'Federal Exhibition of Scientific Achievements' in Moscow, first opened in August 1954 (initially as a 'Farming Exhibition').

New Beginnings

85

191

Uncertainty in questions of taste and style even dominated discussions that took place in the House of the Architect in Moscow in 1968, with the title 'What is disturbing furniture manufacturers?' It stated that in earlier times there was still a clear idea of the means and ways of future furniture design while 'today this clarity has disappeared in proportion to the progress that has taken place'. This comment revealed a longing to return to simple, functional modernity. At the same time, many believed that foreign products could lead society astray: 'while our furniture industry is attempting to liberate itself from all kinds of styles in order to keep up with world standards, these were themselves changing and becoming more complicated'.

Some methods to avoid the crisis were soon seen to be questionable. National and ethnographic elements were part of this. They were taken up by the design, being thought of as 'enlivening' and to a certain extent also being attempts to express the taste of a certain consumer group, returning to heavy, ponderous forms. There was, however, a greater attempt to build diverse gadgets into the furniture and more attention was paid to making it flexible.

190

Consumers had to come to terms with the fact that striving to create greater quantities had negative effects on the quality of furniture. As the industry was dependent on the quantity of contracts and on special demands, there were no possibilities for influencing design and form. Therefore the amount of old-fashioned items increased while a lack of modern artefacts continued. The change in the wishes of

190 River steamboat in the new lock of the Moscow-Volga Canal, early 1950s. Photo: I Shagin. – 191 Badge for the 5th World Youth and Student Games in Moscow, 1957.

the younger generation contributed largely to this imbalance in the relationship between what was on offer and what was in demand. It was mainly the younger people who found the furniture of the fifties and early sixties inappropriate.

As far as the various attempts at finding a system of norms for certain types of furniture was concerned, success remained limited. One of these standardised models was taken up by the furniture industry in the seventies. There were about forty versions for nine different types of kitchens, living rooms and bedrooms. Although the possible combinations were many and their coordination for the dimensions of a modern apartment exact, the work of the designer was limited severely. The recommended rectangular form of the clipboard hardly allowed for artistic design apart from stereotypical decoration. The apartments were all alike, as a result, diverging only in small details. The rectangular contours of the mass-produced products dominated.

192

Experts, however, tried to find ways out of the situation in the course of discussions, as had been the case ten years earlier. Boris Neshumov, a well known furniture designer, made a case for closer coordination between scientists and designers, as the ideas of industry did not correspond to actual living conditions. Moreover, there was no real problem with furniture 'as it is a problem to obtain food.'

Furniture shops and brochures made variations on what had become a single theme – the 'salon' in which one could rest or, should the need arise, eat lunch. There were no desks or bunkbeds for children. It was often pointless to search for sliding doors and furniture that could be folded for small apartments. The arrival in the design world of two young designers, Alexander Sikatshev and Irina Lutshkova, was therefore like a breath of fresh air and even appeared revolutionary. For an exhibition competition, they had created a room with the dimensions of a normal living room whereby the furniture could be, so to say, taken from the walls according to circumstances, as was not designed traditionally in the form of cupboards, shelves or tables. Simple boards were attached to the walls with hinges. They could partially be folded down and, as they had hangers, provided horizontal shelf areas. A room such as this had more

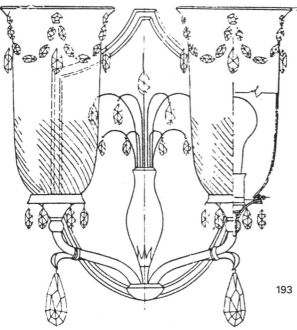

193

192 Abram Damski: chandelier with neon tubes on the Krasniye-Vorota Square in Moscow, 1952.
193 G Lebedev: design for a wall lamp with mirror for two bulbs, 1950.

194

195

196

199

197

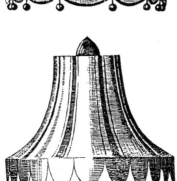

198

194 O Pshenitshnikova: interior of a lounge and dining room, 1950s. – 195 Desk lamp with rabbit-shaped base, 1950s. – 196–198 Lampshades covered by material. 1950. – 199 Dimitri Soanegin: *Mushroom* table lamp, manufactured in the Electrosvet Factory in Moscow since 1950.

88

space, greater working areas and storage spaces for books and musical instruments.

Lutshkova and Sikatshev called their system of mobile elements MEBAR (architectural furniture), which was distinguishable from the usual, standardised, rectangular use of space and was reminiscent of Constructivist experiments. The living room, which could also be used as a workroom, could attain additional dimensions (different from the usual rectangular form) by having diagonal areas, corners and door-openings. The design was highly original, causing architects to discuss it at length. Finally, however, it remained no more than another idea in answer to the always acute question of how the common human need for living space and private cosiness could be more satisfyingly fulfilled other than in row upon row of monotonous concrete blocks in communal settlements, with highly sparse interiors, manufactured in State factories.

Quick answers to this question could hardly be expected from VNIITE. Founded in 1962, after a resolution by the Ministerial Council of the USSR, the Federal Scientific Research Centre for Technological Aesthetics was to look into the general acceptance of methods of 'artistic construction' and also in putting them into practice with a basis of forms and their demands on design. The institute was divided into eight branches in Leningrad, Vilna, Charkov, Sverdlovsk, Baku, Tibilissi, Erevan and Charbarovsk.

What was meant by 'artistic construction' was no more than practical design, while the term

200 N Osterman, N Maunova, A Ovtchinnikov: built-in cupboard shelves in an industrially-produced experimental house, 1952. 201 G Ivanov: cover design for the periodical *Decorative Arts in the Soviet Union,* No 4, 1964. – 202 Abram Damski: standing lamp with table cover, 1960s.

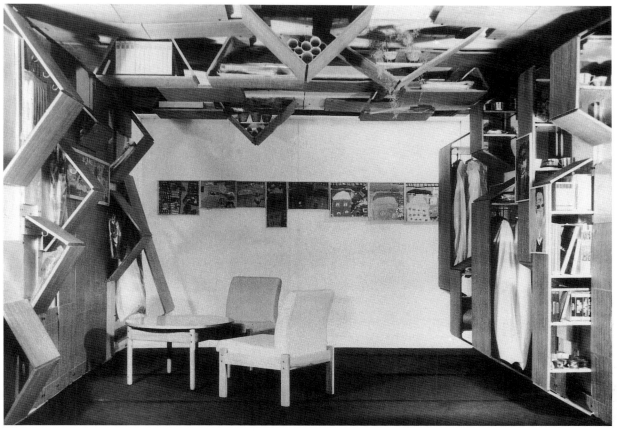

203

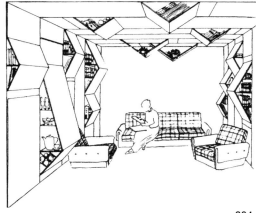
204

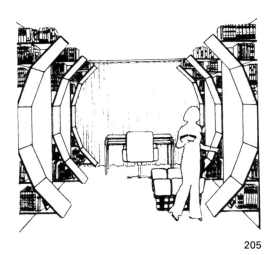
205

203 Alexander Sikatchev, Irina Lutshkova: MEBAR System (architectural furniture), model, 1974. Photo: A Sikatchev. – 204 and 205 Alexander Sikatchev, Irina Lutshkova: drawings for the MEBAR System with diverse possibilities, 1974. – 206 Housing estate in the Kuntsevo area, Moscow, 1970.

207

208

'technological aesthetics' applied to the whole area of scientific research that could make optimal, industrial design possible. They were aiming for a synthesis of science and practical design. At the same time, they wished to research the history of design and methods that could be used, as well as the legitimacy of its impact. The programme also included social, psychological tasks, such as those concentrating on the behaviour of the consumer, his latent wishes and concrete expectations according to the composition of certain goods. Additionally, they attempted to obtain legal norms and standards for designers.

More clarity in this area seemed urgent. The problem was that the designer's work was still both richly diverse and indefinable. The designer could be regarded, with all possible combinations, as artist, technician, engineer or scientific consultant of a project. Yet his position was usually that of an ordinary employee. Apart from exceptional cases, this removed the possibility of creative development, transforming him into a specialist more or less against his will and allowing simmer-

207 Type SIL-130 lorry as a refrigerator lorry, 1960s. – 208 Refrigerators on a conveyor belt in the SIL Factory in Moscow, 1960s.

209

210

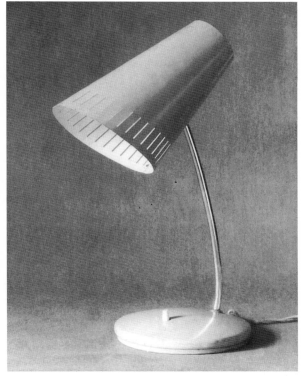

211

209 A type M-22 Volga limousine, early 1960s. – 210 Radio with built-in record-player, model Record-47, manufactured in Berdsk, Siberia, early 1960s. – 211 Table lamp, 1962.

212

213

214

212 Eduard Motshanov: demonstration drawing for a taxi, 1964.
213 and 214 Yuri Dolmatovski, Alexander Olshanetski, Anatoli Tsherniaiev: prototype of the taxi designed by E Motshanov, 1965–66, and view of the interior.

215

216

ing energies to remain below the surface. This resulted in many designers leaving the field of production in order to work as freelance graphic and design artists. They had high aims and there was hope that the standards of Soviet design would soon be raised. These expectations were held all the more as the VNIITE also trained designers itself and advertised its goals.

After the VCHUTEMAS-VCHUTEIN was closed in 1930, there was no central organisation that could train industrial designers in a truly successful manner. The field was dominated mainly by architects and engineers. The members of recently opened regional design offices were often enthusiastic although they frequently lacked specialised knowledge.

Designs for a taxi (1963-65) were amongst the experimental projects initiated by the VNIITE. The car was built in the institute's workshops and had various noteworthy, new elements. The bodywork was made of synthetic material. It was reinforced by fibreglass while the interior was reinforced with plywood. The interior was furnished in imitation plastic, covered by material. The seats, steering wheel and panelling all appeared highly modern. The engine was in the rear while wide, sliding doors provided the passenger with a comfort-

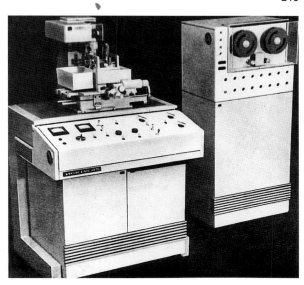

217

215 Yuri Polikarpov, Alexei Safonov: electric drilling-machine, *Kama* model, 1970s. – 216 W Wintman, G Sokolovski and others: tractor, design for production in the Mogilev Factory, 1962–63. – 217 Alexander Grashin, Alexander Melnikov and others: electric turning bench, 1970s.

218

219

220

221

able mode of entering and exiting the vehicle. The VNIITE periodical, *Technological Aesthetics*, discussed the model at length, comparing it with the serially produced Volga car that was also used as a taxi at the time. The illustrations alone already showed that the new car had more comfortable seats and a more functional boot. Additionally, there were the advantages that had appeared when both models were tried under similar conditions. It was easier to use, having better driving qualities and greater economic advantages. This user-friendly car, however, was never built, as was the case with milling machines, radios and other technical gadgets developed by the experimental workshops of the VNIITE in following years (from initial model to models ready to be manufactured).

The causes of this lay mainly, as was so often the case, in the infexibility of State administration, with its centralised structures and the manner in which the abilities found within the planning apparatus of ministries overlapped. They paralysed one another and failed to understand the ideas of technically and artistically gifted designers (providing these had actually managed to reach them). Usually several years passed between the finished product deisgn and its realisation, a time span that often made the first sample outdated for new aims in the planned economy (unless necessary improvements were made). The arms industry and space travel always took precedence.

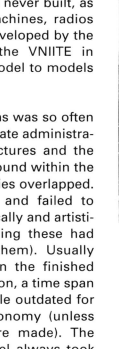

222

218 The Apollo-Soyus Spaceships in linked-up condition before the Exhibition of Scientific and Technical Inventions in Moscow, 1985. – 219 Military Office: transportation helicopter, Mi-10 model, 1970s. – 220 Spacesuit, 1970s.

221 Fedor Pribyshtshenko, Oleg Frolov and others: *Meteor* hydrofoil, 1960s. – 222 Electric lock of the VL series, using alternating current, 1970s.

223

224

223 Lev Kutsmitchev, Vladimir Ariamov, Alexander Olshanetski: prototype of a fire-engine, 1974. – 224 Lev Kutsmitchev, Vladimir Ariamov, Alexander Olshanetski: model of a fire-engine with fire ladder, 1973–74.

225 Dmitri Asrikan, Piotr Alexeiev and others: suitcases and other bags for electrical measuring devices from the *Soyuselectropribor,* 1980–81. – 226 *Electromera* logo of the *Soyuselectropribor* series of devices. – 227 Computer-driven switchboard with screen from the *Soyuselectropribor* programme. – 228 Switchboard of the *Soyuselectropribor* programme. – 229 Computer working space with possibilities for extension from the *Soyuselectropribor* programme.

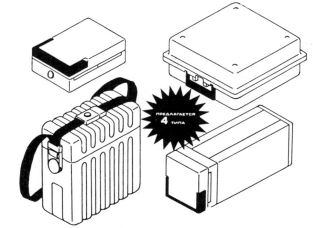

ЭЛЕКТРО∧ЕРА

226

228

225

техническая эстетика
9/1981
ISSN 0136-5363

227

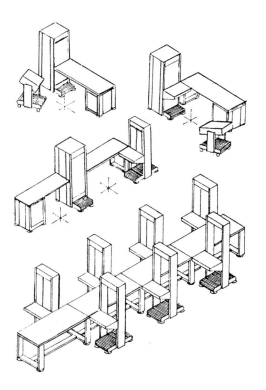

229

230

The Seventies and Eighties

Despite the difficulties encountered, the VNIITE had at least partially realised a number of larger projects and had brought about a deeper understanding of the manifold tasks of industrial design in the public. It was no longer a priority to create models. Designers took greater part in the planning of individual industrial branches. Additionally, they had the opportunity to help design working areas in factories, influence factory halls and installation of machinery, design interiors of break areas and style working clothes. The so-called Design Programme was particularly effective as a method of influencing design and, as was stated in the periodical, *Technological Aesthetics,* 'solving...the problems of realisation with socio-cultural standards'. Behind this lay the wish for a 'total design' – completely new designs for larger factories which would be uniform. Working areas for engineers and other employees, uniforms, graphic symbols, production methods, the use of gadgets, workshops and laboratories, the entire contents should all adhere to a uniformly constructed form that focused on production

231

232

230 V Gorbatchev, S Larina: T-40 AM tractor, 1978. – 231 V Blagorasumov, V W Umniashkin and others: IZH-2126 car, prototype for production at the Ishevsk Factory, 1978–79. – 232 V Blagorasumov, V Saveliev: small car for children, *IZH Buggy,* 1979.

233

234

235

233 Kamov Design Studio: KA-26 helicopter, 1970s. – 234 Marc Demidovtshev: PAZ *Tourist-lux* bus, built in the Pavlova Bus Factory, 1970s. – 235 VNIITE Design Studio in the Urals: tram, 1970s.

methods and functionality, although reaching beyond a conversion of existing elements.

The Union Electrical Measuring Instrument Factory was chosen as experimental ground for the enormous 'Design Programme'. Even the presentation of a primary, 'complex' design unleashed a great controversy. Several critics believed that the demands of the entire programme would diminish the quality of the individual designs and would reduce the effects of some useful preliminary work. Others found the whole project questionable because it had been vociferously advised to restrict itself to factories still at the planning stage (rather than concern itself with those already in existence).

As far as the propagation of the programme was concerned, the critics were right. Slogans on the institute walls promoted it, therefore influencing the working atmosphere in the buildings themselves, contributing little to the objectivity of research that should defend the entire project with scientific criteria. It was therefore not surprising that the majority of documents disappeared from the ministries without ever again seeing the light of day. Had the 'Design Programme' therefore failed as a whole?

It only gradually became apparent in the case of the Union Electrical Measuring Instrument Factory. On the other hand, it proved helpful in the development of visual communication, such as when the old airport system was being replaced by a more modern one. It played little role in furniture design although it

236

237

238

had an unusually indirect influence on concepts of uniform, decoration of cultural centres, restaurants, cafés and museums. The wish for totality on a huge scale and the wish to affect organisational structures of companies brought more doubt and discredit than credit for the programme. Seen from today's point of view, it appears (despite some positive aspects) symptomatic of the method of planning with its own laws, and removed from the reality that was inherent in the bureaucracies of authoritarian states.

Besides 'official' designers, under State control, design developed within the Artists Association (where many furniture, ceramic and textile designers had come together) relatively freely in the sixties and seventies. It is hard to judge the wide-ranging spectrum of work objectively – conventional forms and patterns outweighed original ideas. Moreover, there were usually only small numbers of artefacts that were manufactured. Exclusively decorative objects often looked like craft kitsch. This had already found success during the Stalin era, as a 'subculture' with folkloristic elements, or symbolism that idealised more or less insistent Socialist ideas and 'achievements' – all of which had little to do with artistic design.

A rediscovery of early Russian design of the twenties took place slowly during the Khruschev era (excluding the public to a certain extent) with its 'spring' period of 'de-Stalinisation', economic reforms and free coexistence. As far as cultural politics was concerned, the new polycentrism did not include dismis-

236 Alexander Ermolaiev, Igor Beresovski and others: models of the exhibits in the foyer of the Russia Hotel in Moscow on the occasion of the congress of the umbrella organisation of the International Design Councils (ICSID), 1975. – 237 Yevgeni Bogdanov demonstrates the cardboard information stand developed by his team for the ICSID Congress in Moscow, 1975. – 238 Design for a visual communication method for the ICSID Congress.

239

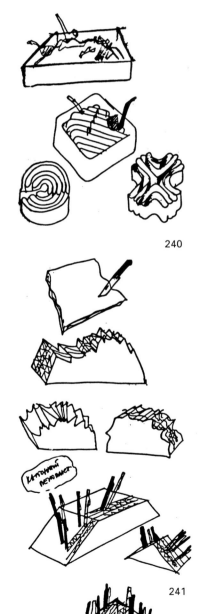

240

242

241

239 Badges for participants of
the ICSID Congress. – 240 Design
sketches for a cardboard ashtray.
241 Design sketches for cardboard writing equipment. –
242 Seating with cardboard
elements for participants of the
ICSID Congress.

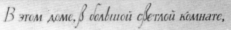

В этом доме, в большой светлой комнате,

жил маленький старичок.

243

ИСКУССТВО
КНИГИ
'65/66

244

sal of the theory of class war or the bad influence of the 'class enemy' in the West. Furthermore there were possibilities for obtaining information that were greater and more diverse than had been the case in the fifties. American designers such as Raymond Loewy were also known in the Soviet Union. It was therefore more difficult to accept that a whole era of Russian art and design was treated negatively, if not denied completely, as if it was an embarrassing period with achievements one should retrospectively be ashamed of.

The colleges for industrial design were the main training grounds for aspiring designers. The curricula, created in 1966, were based on experiences from the teaching methods of the VCHUTEMAS-VCHUTEIN. They divided the discipline into three groups: artistic design (drawing, painting, composition, sculpture), practical construction (materials, working techniques, engineering) and theory (art history, history and theory of design, politics and social sciences). The Moscow school could look back to a long classical, academic tradition, particularly in the fields of architecture and graphic design. Most of the graduates from the Faculty of Architectural Design, opened at the Architectural Institute in Sverdlovsk in 1969, went to work in car factories or for similar State companies, important for further economic development.

245

243 Victor Pivovarov: double page with illustrations from a children's book (*The Large and the Small*), 1978. – 244 Maxim Shukov, Arkadi Troianker: cover design for the *Book Art Yearbook,* 1970. – 245 V Umnov: product emblem, 1960s.

ЗНАНИЕ-СИЛА

ЗНАНИЕ·СИЛА

246

247

248

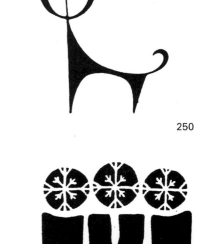

250

249

251

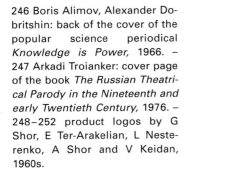

252

246 Boris Alimov, Alexander Do-
britshin: back of the cover of the
popular science periodical
Knowledge is Power, 1966. –
247 Arkadi Troianker: cover page
of the book *The Russian Theatrical Parody in the Nineteenth and
early Twentieth Century,* 1976. –
248–252 product logos by G
Shor, E Ter-Arakelian, L Neste-
renko, A Shor and V Keidan,
1960s.

253

254

In 1975, a conference of the International Council of Societies of Industrial Design (ICSID), was held at the Rossia Hotel in Moscow (it was initiated by VNIITE). It was important in several ways. Firstly, it was not controlled by cultured ministerial bureaucrats, as was the case with comparable events. Secondly, it offered opportunities for meeting guests from numerous countries and presenting the best designs that had been created in the USSR in recent years. The congress motto 'Design for Man and Society' was not only interesting for Soviet participants. Centrally important, however, was the exchange of experiences and the discussion of concrete plans, using exhibited plans and objects.

The exhibited samples from the Soviet Union were, on the whole, respectable, constructive forms, made of modest materials, easy to service and use and for the most part avoiding decorative elements. The easy manageability and uncomplicated assembling of spare parts created objects whose final form would be determined by the consumer himself when he put them together. Diagrams and posters (some by the photo-designer, Igor Beresovski), information leaflets and films were additions to a programme richly filled with lectures and discussions. Significantly, however, it was precisely those members of VNIITE who had organised this international designer conference and had created the concept, that left the institute. Beresovski became a freelance graphic artist, Yevgeni Bogdanov found a new career as an exhibition organiser, Alexander Ermolaiev became a teacher and Viktor Senkov turned to film. The

255

256

253 Viatsheslav Shpak: podium design for the 'Celebration of the 60th Anniversary of the Founding of the USSR' in Moscow, Congress Palace, 1987. Photo: W Evstigneiev. – 254 Viatsheslav Shpak, I Vinogradskiu and others: decorations and stands for the Olympic Fire at the Olympic Games in Moscow, 1980. Photo: W Evstigneiev.

255 Sports parade at the Olympic Games in Moscow, 1980. Photo: V Evstigneiev. – 256 Vassili Akopov, Mikhail Anikst, Valeri Diakonov, Alexander Krukov, Ivan Tikhomirov, Boris Trofimov, Alexander Shumilin: designs for pictogrammes for the Olympic Games in Moscow, 1980.

problem was the conflict between their own creativity and the mediocrity ordained from above; between personal, highly creative initiatives and the jungle of official, although unwritten, directives, behind which the all-powerful cultural bodies hid themselves, as if behind a protective wall.

This conflict affected all areas of Soviet society. Its roots and all the deformities it caused – reflected in the fates of both individuals and whole groups – reached far back to the Stalin era. Today, the end of its influence still cannot be gauged. Taking away individual responsibility was only part of this, as was the incompetence of those who had economic and public power in their hands. The dilemma was not the misuse of power but the fact that this power became so total that any complaints were, so to say, strangled at birth, provided they even managed to get a hearing during decades of inflexible mechanisms.

It was an almost everyday procedure that design projects, as soon as initial steps were taken, were constantly examined, altered or dismissed in favour of less demanding designs. Applied graphic art had an easier time of it. Due to the pressure of narrower time limits, it had more freedom. It could also react more quickly and flexibly (with poster advertising, for example) to contracts from industry and State trading companies. Although sometimes consciously catering to the taste of the masses, it also had an educational function for the aesthetic ideas of all potential consumers. Techniques such as photomontage and collage (used by Rodchenko in such a wonderful

257   258

manner) which had been neglected for a long time, enjoyed a renaissance. At the same time, the layout of several publications became more lively. There was a general attempt at creating visually attractive, interesting design, as well as a higher standard of printing.

There was no distinct hierarchical difference between 'higher' and 'lower' graphic design, if the former were to be designated to theatre or film posters and the latter to names of goods or company logos. The attention span for these could be sustained in equal measure and the aesthetic design was equally original. When the USSR Council of Ministers published a resolution that forced each factory to have its own, officially registered trading emblem in 1962, graphic artists had an enormous amount of work throughout the Soviet Union. More than 200,000 emblems had to be designed in a short period of time. The need for simple and appropriate designs was met by noteworthy designs, the best of which were published in the periodicals *Decorative Art in the USSR* and *Technological Aesthetics*.

The fact that graphic artists – amongst them some that were well known – were concerned with such banalities as product packaging, designing company logos and thinking about psychological aspects that aid consumption

259

257 Alexander Vrona, Yektarina Lapina and others: *Tom-206* tape-recorder with radio, with removeable loudspeakers, 1979. – 258 Vladimir Anisimov: *Astra* tape-recorder, 1970. – 259 Alexei Koshelev: exhibits from the exhibition Product Design Vouching For Quality, 1975. Photo: N Moshkin.

260 J. Vorobdshev, S. Bogatyrev, A. Brodin: *Comfort* hoover, with removeable case and extension parts, 1979. – 261 Irina Presnetsova, Alexei Chauke: heater on the floor and on a stand, 1978.

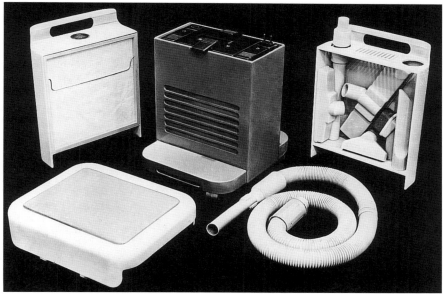

260

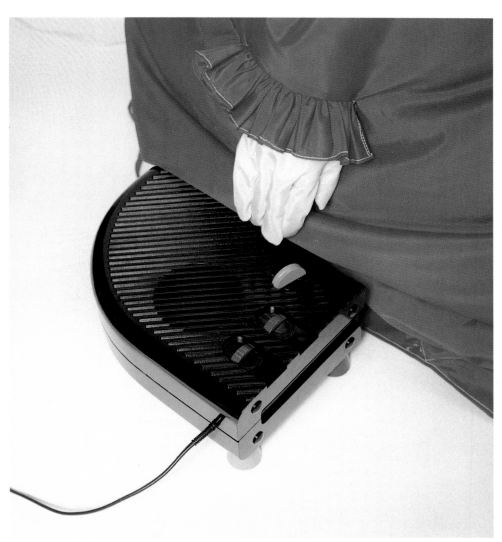

261

was already a sign (for some colleagues) that a new type of career with its own theoretical concept was coming into existence. This was naturally formulated in an entirely different area, that of semiotics and information theory (and only recently, in 1991). Graphic design, wrote the theoretician, Sergei Serov 'transforms information into visual signals that can be clearly interpreted'. This, however, only applied to a small amount of the designs created in the seventies and eighties. It was only after the emergence of pictogrammes that the relationship between information and image, or sign, became more clear – signs replaced the written word. Before this, it was not possible to forego words, despite all attempts at arriving at formulae that were as succinct and symbolic as possible and described a product, its composition and origin clearly, possibly also its usage.

It therefore took a while before the term 'graphic design' was defined precisely, resulting from conclusions that are still questioned today. At first, it had been placed on the same footing as black-and-white photography. Specific occasions and purpose played a rather minor role – designing a box for sweets was not so different to designing a book jacket. Attempts at achieving greater variety were made, due to the diverse ways products were used, going hand in hand with progress

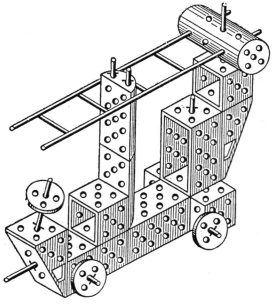

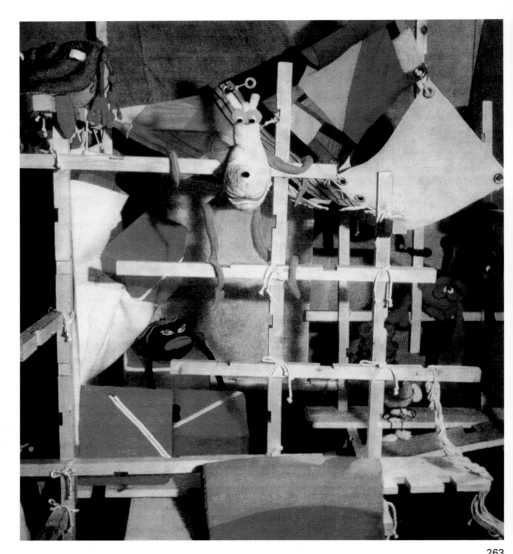

262

263

264

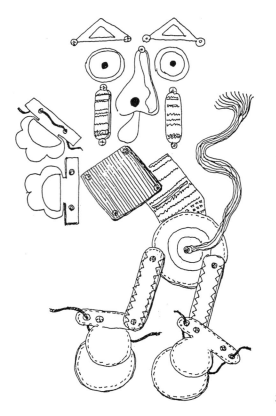

265

262 V Polikarpov: toy fire-engine, made of large blocks, 1943.

263 Irina Presnetsova: convertible scenery for kindergarten theatre productions, 1976–77.

264 Alexander Ermolaiev, Tatiana Rubtshova: EPO-KSI blocks for contruction by children, 1976.

265 Irina Presnetsova: pattern with parts of a lion costume for children's theatre, 1976.

266

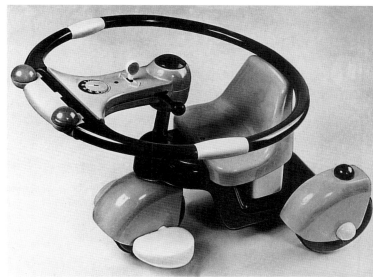

267

268

in these areas and were linked to what was to become a rejection of the stylistic ideals of Socialist Realism. Film posters from around 1960, which also created a stir abroad, had reached beyond coventions that had been cultivated for years with unimpeded freshness. Significantly, it was often imported Western films that gave poster designers the courage to reach out to new formal methods.

The programme developed by VNIITE to create a company style (or corporate identity system) widened the scope of the designer in such a way that applied graphic design became only a part of a field of tasks that was to become more and more complex. The word 'design' was used in the context of shows that were designed and choreographed for the masses and for all public events that needed aesthetic forms. The pompous opening ceremony at the 1980 Olympic Games in Moscow was such an event. The way the city was decorated on this occasion, the information booths, the clothes of the hostesses, the countless pictogrammes that appeared to achieve a wordless dialogue with the viewer, as they faced him, the English signs on the underground stations, all demonstrated perfect organisation although it did not arouse a completely enthusiastic response as the same form – or similar forms – were repeated endlessly, thus creating a certain monotony.

266 Alexander Lavrentiev: building block, 1976. – 267 V Kruglikov, B Petrov: electric car for children, 1977. – 268 Elena Yasykova: interior climbing-frame in the form of four figures, 1980.

New Methods and Perspectives

Inspired by the Moscow ICSID Congress of 1975, teachers and designers discovered an area of modern design that had not received much attention for a long time: the design of toys. Students and graduates were the first to design new toys.

Scientific, didactic studies provided the theoretical framework and it was recalled that the first kindergarten building blocks had been patented by Polikarpov in the Soviet Union in 1943. His system, later variated and also taken over by West European countries, was based on a simple principle – children should learn to play constructively and imaginatively by building miniature structures at an early age with blocks of various sizes.

An experimental construction kit was created by A Ermolaiev, T Rubchova and A Simonova in the VNIITE in 1976. Children could play with this and also experience real situations or create environments according to suggested themes such as 'Africa', 'Summer in the Environs of Moscow' or could make objects from everyday life – like cars. The attraction of the construction kit lay in its manifold possibilities for combining things, allowing a child's imagination to be mobilised in many directions. One of the designers commented that one should learn to see the world through the eyes of a toddler. Most things surrounding a child are dumb and soulless – 'children cannot understand how they function and how they are constructed.' Educational games, for which the construction kit was highly suited, would make it easier to deal with the world. 'The child perceives the world only by imitating his surroundings, whether these are natural or artificial, living or mechanical, simple or complicated, understandable or secretive . . .' (A Ermolaiev).

The objects provided by the construction kit imitated the natural qualities of real things. Stylised abstractions or purely functional forms were consciously rejected. According to the age group for which they were meant, other projects departed from the principle of playful imitation. As the child's way of perceiving was studied, new design possibilities could be developed, even if many designs were not realised.

Plans and models were created within the framework of the teaching programme of the Soviet Artists' Group in the seventies and eighties under the umbrella term 'artistic design'. Being purely experimental, the designs were meant to inspire projects that were already far advanced, to aid aesthetic education and to bring about public discussions, as far as was possible.

Even if the artistic designs were regarded only superficially and from the outside, the main ideas and aims were soon recognisable. In short, more stress was placed on the creative component inherent in any type of design. More importance was placed on individual, creative talents and design itself was to be unified with common aesthetic human needs. Was design therefore an artificially produced by-product of Constructivism that had redesigned even the most banal of objects in a revolutionary manner?

Evgeni Rosenblium became the most famous leader of artistic design. His book *Artists in Design* is both a methodology and a discussion of his experiences, explaining the theoretical, as well as setting out a programme and demonstrating how to make experiments. Rosenblum writes that his book 'discusses experiments, at the same time as being a part of these'. Progression and contents of seminars organised by Rosenblium at the Artists' Association, attended by artists from all Soviet Republics, are described. Of central importance is always a project that was created collectively. The teaching method aided the setting aside of a number of pressures that usually had negative, rather than positive, effects on the completion of designs. The artists also learned how to deal with highly diverse materials and became familiar with the main characteristics of modern marketing. After the seminar was over, the fictitious client, which could be a company, Party urban committee or professional body, received a photo or a model of the design – the re-

269

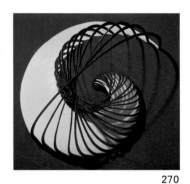

270

271

designing of an urban centre, a company hall, a museum or an interior was often the case. The designs were published and explained by the project leaders, the participants receiving a diploma, stating that they had completed the seminar successfully.

Rosenblium's work was greatly supported by colleagues such as Viatsheslav Glasitshev, Oleg Genisaretski, Larissa Shadova, Karl Kantor and Marc Konik. The book clearly reveals which of the two directions and design methods described should be given priority. He differentiates between scientifically based 'artistic construction' and the creation of the work of art, based on the personal talents of the designer and the degree to which he has learned highly diverse methods. Rosenblium believes that all objects should be produced by highly mechanised modern industry, at the same time as allowing people to 'remain in contact with their own individuality'.

He therefore attributes qualities to the product that enobles it to a certain degree, lifting it out of the everyday world, on condition that the consumer sense of aesthetics and general cultural needs are met, instead of alienation. Rosenblium, however, adds that 'designing objects according to the consumer's wishes reveals little about the artist's creative imagination.' The consumer is not just any 'abstract, ordinary person'. He belongs to a cer-

269 Senez Studio (project leaders: Mark Kronik, Yevgeni Rosenblium): Museum of Space, 1978.
270 Three-dimensional spiral-shaped form, made by Alexander Pushkarev's students at the Textile Institute in Moscow, 1987.
271 Senez Studio (project leaders: Mark Kronik, Yevgeni Rosenblium, Andrei Bokov, Andrei Skokan): sketch for re-designing Deribasovskaia St. in Odessa, 1977.

272

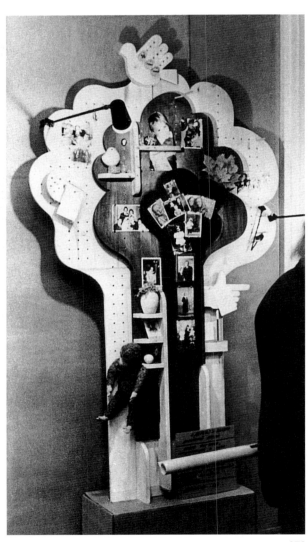

273

274

272 Opening of the First Exhibition of Young Designers in Moscow, 1976. – 273 Leonti Osernikov: *The Tree of Memory*, picture and shelf part, 1976. – 274 View into the First Exhibition of Young Designers in Moscow with pneumatic lamps by Mikhail Borissov, an armchair by Stanislav Chermenski in the background, 1976. Photo: I Beresovski.

275

276

tain group, in age and cultural experience, having a specific level of education, as well as certain beliefs and prejudices. It was therefore all the more necessary for design to take the most diverse consumer needs into account.

Rosenblium's book was published in 1974, contributing to the aesthetic design in the Soviet Union and bringing about greater public discussion of design. Designers, as well as architects and visual artists hoped to give the 'creation of the work of art' the status it had lost in the mass production and standardisation since the thirties. The largely experimental (as well as partly functional) character of designs allowed untapped creativity to come to the fore, even bringing highly individual and daring projects into existence. An underground cultural centre, a cosmos museum, a cultural centre in faraway Jelabuga (dedicated to the poet, Marina Svetaieva), the reconstruction of the Deribasovskaia Street in Odessa and other similar projects were planned. Each detail could inspire new variations.

The models created under the aegis of the Artists' Association had the autonomy of a work of art, although they contained enough ideas for future planning and kept close to reality. This autonomy was naturally not durable because the materials used were usually suit-

275 Yevgeni Bogdanov: *Afternoon Snack* ceramic set, 1975–76. – 276 Alexander Ermolaiev: furniture in the brutalist style, 1976.

able only for exhibitions that would not be permanent. The meticulously assembled paper and cardboard pieces were destroyed almost as soon as they were created. Whether this was a model of a tractor or an architectural ensemble remained unimportant. Their lifespan was short, as was indicated by the labels given to this highly transitory design method – 'paper designs' or 'paper design'.

'Paper architecture' was a similar term. This was conceptual architectural design, concerning a theme, rather than a concrete building. Architects taking part in international competitions created these. 'Paper' meant that the construction of specific buildings was ruled out.

On the whole, it was the young artists who believed in the idea of paper design (creating what can almost be described as a movement). They presented themselves to the public for the first time in 1976, with the First Exhibition of Young Designers in Moscow. This took place under the aegis of the Artists' Association, whereby there was a stress on the solidarity of professional designers, for the most part graduates of the former Stroganov Art School, with participants of seminars in the Studio for Artistic Design. Although this exhibition showed objects that could be not be strictly termed 'paper design', most designs demonstrated unusually great creativity and sometimes even had visionary characteristics. The fact that the designer should be able to use highly diverse materials and realise his own ideas entered the sphere of simply creative experimentation (as should have naturally been the case). Therefore, not simply designs, but objects created after them, were shown at the exhibition, amongst them glazed ceramics (E Bogdanov), wooden furniture (A Ermolaiev) and lamps (M Borisov).

The central theme of the exhibition was the apartment, its furniture, and its function in everyday life. Several designers had amused themselves by designing small models while others exhibited their art with its original

277

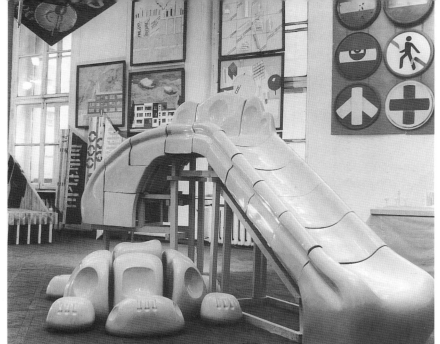

278

279

280

278 Alexander and Gennadi Vrosov: ceramic slide from the exhibition 'Design for a City', 1978. – 279 Room with new objects (*A City Shawl* by Irina Presnetsova, wooden bench by Yuri Nasarov) from the exhibition 'Design for a City', 1978. –

280 Alexander Ermolaiev: suggestions for re-designing the cityscape, colours for housing estates, 'Design for a City' exhibition, 1978.

dimensions. A chair by S Chermenski largely consisted of an aluminium frame with side parts which had a great deal of space for small objects in sewed-on pockets. The whole was conceived as a comfortable 'nest', as 'apartment within an apartment' for purposes of reflection, reading or listening to music. There was also an ensemble that 'could be transformed' with cushions, and records that could be combined at will, creating new 'landscapes for living.' The EPO-KSI Construction Kit with bricks, blocks, bits of material and mattresses had similar functions. What emerged again and again was the intention of rejecting the idea of furniture as being passive. An attempt was made to create objects to which one could relate in a more lively way, even if this meant no more than occasionally 'composing' the ensemble in a new manner.

The second exhibition, held in 1978, was of different dimensions, its theme being 'Design for a City.' There were ten architects among the twenty-eight participants. This was due to the self-chosen task of developing alternatives to large building projects and relieving the uniform grey of the city with livelier accents. The city was to become more attractive – even if only partially – more friendly and easy to live in. The plan for redesigning the city centre by Evgeni Ass and Vladislav Kirpitshev, a stand for advertising and showing new products, a ceramic slide and house-numbers of the same material were only some of the unorthodox advances in the direction of making the city more attractive, even if they could only be of a cosmetic nature.

The exhibition held two years previously had enabled a reversal of the situation Russian designers of the twenties had found themselves in. The technological prerequisites for serial and mass production of products according to examples and models had still been in their initial stages – except for textiles and graphics. It was the technology of modern mass production, however, that now provided artists with a way of realising their ideas. They used this widely without losing originality in the designs. Additionally, creative imagination helped them to invent objects that would probably never exist in reality.

It was also not difficult to see that the majority of the exhibits of the second exhibition were created with artistic liberty. One of the participants, I Presnetsova, described her work in

281

282

283

281 Boris Mikhailov: colourful elements of window displays and house number signs made of ceramics for Starosadski Street in Moscow, 'Design for a City' exhibition, 1978. – 282 Leonid Jentus, Igor Maistrovski and others: parts of a project for re-designing main shopping and traffic streets in Moscow, 1978.

283 Victor Senkov: advertising boards with the BIM module system for green areas in delapidated urban areas. Apart from new plants, the project includes the creation of new paths, hills and areas of water, 1978.

284 Senez Studio (project leader: Yevgeni Rosenblum): suggestions for re-designing streets in Tshernovitz, Ukraine, 1986.

284

285

286

287

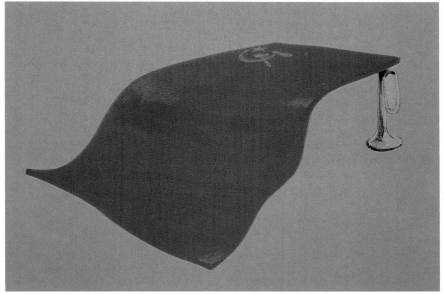

288

the following manner: 'While designing I am free as a bird'. An article written about the exhibition explained that 'the designers are exhibiting designs, not products'. Objects that revealed the work of an original mind created the greatest stir. Factors such as the combination of colours, optical qualities, the composition, weight and even smell of the material were taken into account. Presentation was equally important. While models and graphic designs dominated at the first exhibition of young designers, it was construction, installations and three-dimensional forms with a multitude of cross-references that were meant to express the designer's ideas in the second. Such 'stage designs' found general approval and once again underlined the artistic nature of the exhibits.

Exhibits by Alexander Ermolaiev, one of the exhibition organisers, demonstrated the degree in which the second Moscow exhibition had moved beyond traditional ideas about the nature and function of design. He was primarily concerned with the perception of material qualities, and the manner in which people react to matter in general, as can be observed in his teaching and designs for children's building block systems. 'Material' included fragments, the remains of objects, ugly after being overused and things that had been thrown away, such as rubbish bins. Ermolaiev was an outsider amongst the Russian designers of his generation, aesthetising partially destroyed objects, found by chance.

289

285 Yevgeni Bogdanov, Stanislav Tshermenski, Yuri Avakumov: installation in the exhibition 'Mayakovsky and Production Art' in Moscow, K Melnikov's pavilion at the Paris Exhibition of 1925, reconstructed according to the scale 1:5, 1984. – 286 'Exhibition in Honour of Mikhail Bulgakov's 100th Birthday' at the Theatrical Museum in Moscow, 1991. – 287 Yevgeni Bogdanov, Stanislav Chermenski, Yuri Avakumov: installation in the exhibition Mayakovsky and Production Art at the Mayakovsky Museum in Moscow, demonstration of composing verses, 1984.

288 Nadeshda Averianova: table shaped like the Soviet State flag with a trumpet as leg, 1990. 289 Alexander Lavrentiev: photo chair, 1986.

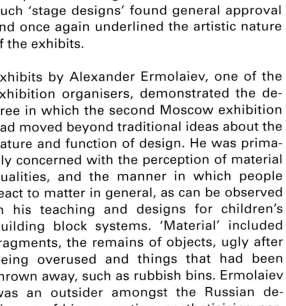

290

290 Installation with photos by Igor Beresovski, radio and telephone by Yuri Solotov, ceramic tea-set by Alexander Ermolaiev and Gennadi Vrosvov, from the exhibition 'The Design Artist', 1988. – 291 Olga Pobetova: dress with printed advertising, 1988.

291

292

292 Vladimir Chaika: logo of the exhibition 'The Design Artist', 1988. – 293 View of the exhibition 'The Design Artist' with hanging musical objects by Viatcheslav Koleitchak, photos by Francisco Infante, and the competition model of a train compartment, 1988.

293

294

295

296

294 Viatcheslav Koleitchak: *Almost-Costume,* 1990. – 295 Viatcheslav Koleitchak: spatial composition Mebius-9, 1976. – 296 Viatcheslav Koleitchak: part of the *Almost-Costume* – headpiece as metal and material construction, 1990.

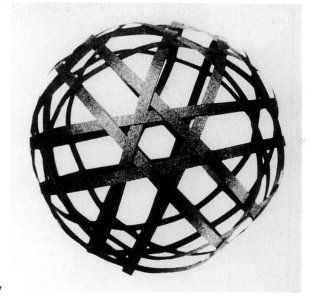

297

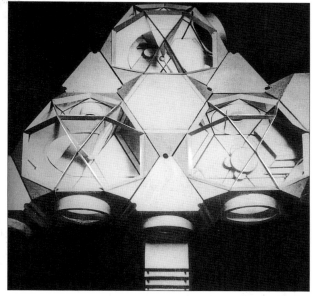

298

However, it cannot be denied that astonishing results were achieved when furniture and toys were actually brought into production, surprising many theoreticians of traditional design.

A plan for a further exhibition of experimental design in the early eighties never came to fruition. This was to show 'realistic design'. Ermolaiev's concept, however, tended to stray in the opposite direction of what could be termed 'realism'. Once again, 'unusual objects that have a high artistic and aesthetic value' were to be seen, with appeals being made to the wealth of ideas and imagination of each participant. Some of the phrasing revealed that the exhibition was at least indirectly counteracting all types of mass production and the manner in which consumers had grown accustomed to the mechanisms of industrial production. Materials and technological methods were limited in nature. The term 'realistic' could only make some sense in connection with looking at the past, without losing touch with reality.

Ermolaiev's ideas were later taken up by several exhibitions on non-traditional design which had themes such as 'Children Draw – Adults Design' or 'The Poetry of Chance'. The Moscow Design Centre took part in an exhibition Ermolaiev helped to organise. Showcases exhibited more than 300 pieces, assembled according to functionality, as well as to the manner in which they had been created: furniture, lamps, carpets, toys, and geometric objects, painted black-and-white or made simply to be touched. What made this exhibition special were the public sites at underground

299

297 Oleg Bodnar: spatial composition, made of tyres, 1970s. – 298 Oleg Bodnar: model of a spatial construction, made of triangular parts and parts with six sides, prototype of mobile architecture, 1970s. – 299 Oleg Bodnar: model of a housing block structure, made of shifted parts, 1970s.

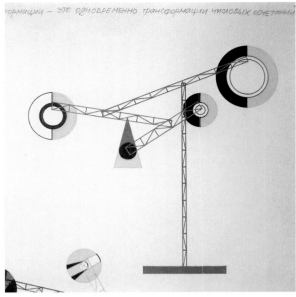

300

entrances. The contents of the showcases provided topics of conversation for the crowds surrounding them on a daily basis (if too demanding, there were questions and guessing games). The exhibition title, 'The Design Artist', naturally placed designer and artist on the same level. This meant that the designer was being considered in a better light. Additionally, combining both functions clarified the task of art to influence the design of everyday objects actively, as had been the case in the twenties.

This was connected to the question whether good design had not always been created by artists rather than professional designers. Looking back, the first one-and-a-half years after the October Revolution, as well as developments in Western European countries, would appear to confirm this. Apart from architects, it was mainly artists and sculptors who provided important impulses for industrial design, the so-called culture of the everyday and general questions of taste. Italy was an example of this. Looking more closely, however, it was obvious that, despite worldwide acclaim and sigificant export success, the 'Italian style' was only seldom connected to mass production. Moreover, quality work could be produced both by artists and professional designers. An 'artistic', aesthetically

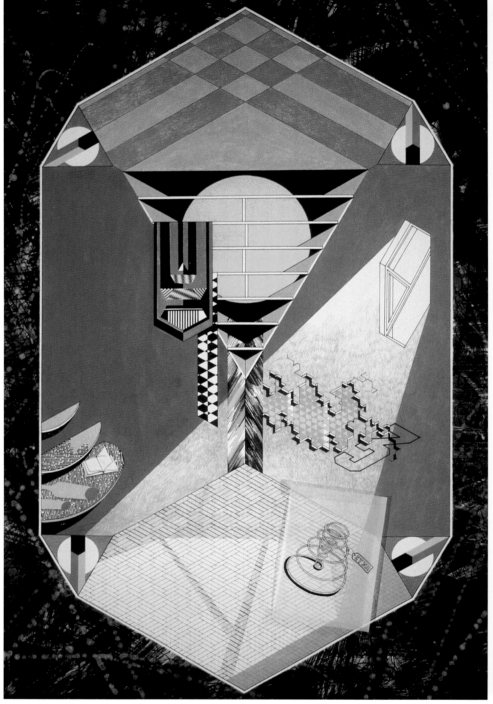

301

300 Alexander Pushkarev: kinetic standing lamp, 1987. – 301 Alexander Pushkarev: design for a kinetic standing lamp, 1987.

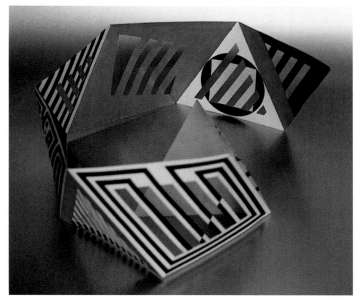

302

pleasing form could easily emerge from the design office of a company. Not all questions raised by the aforementioned exhibitions received definitively clear answers in the following period. What was more important was that the problems of design were being given fresh consideration. This included the changing relationships between model, producer and consumer and the effect the design product had on the way people thought, as well as its role in changing the environment. It was therefore no coincidence that the title of another exibition, at the Mars Gallery in Moscow, promised to shed light on 'contemporary ideas in art'. What was meant by this was a widening of traditional concepts of art and design. Additionally, it attempted shedding light on a world that had grown complicated for Soviet society. Experiments threatened to become autonomous and self-serving, without completely losing touch with reality.

Several more recent developments in the tradition of 'paper design' specifically draw on experimentation, calling this the basis of all creativity. V Gamaionov, V Koleitshak, M Litvinov, O Bodnar, as well as other architects, artists and designers therefore used geometric and stereometric elementary forms in order to explore these possibilities. They made toy-like imaginary architecture, made of

303

302 Alexander Pushkarev: spatial decorative forms, 1988. – 303 Students from the Moscow Textile Institute (project leader: Alexander Pushkarev): decorative spatial structures, 1988–89.

304

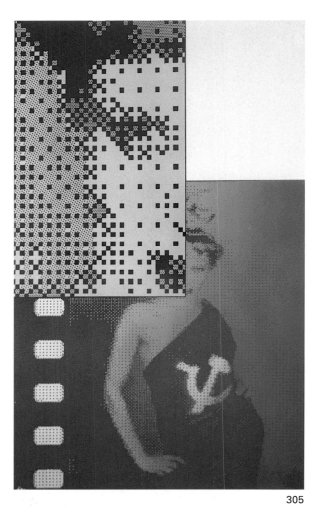

305

cylinders, spatial spirals and further similar shapes, utopian projections of an imaginary future, created under contemporary conditions. Others experimented with computer graphics (A Andreiev, D Abrikosov, A Toponov) or worked with kinetic objects. Bulat Galeiev and his co-workers at the *Prometei* construction studio, named after a work by the Russian composer, Alexander Skriabin, were influenced by the idea of a synthesis of light, colour and sound. They were amongst the first whose work reacted to the invention of calculators.

Courses for experimental work at the art schools, and exhibitions, whose titles were often already a challenge for the public, the work of 'free' experimental groups under the aegis of the State Artists' Association – a change in the climate of cultural politics, taking place in the Soviet Union since the early seventies (at first limited to the large cities) – was present at all of these. This was a difficult process, often destroyed, interrupted and slowed down and cannot be separated from internal political events such as the creation of a new constitution (1976). It began in the sixties with the Samizdat Movement's demands for greater liberalisation. Reactions to exhibitions of contemporary Polish and 'capitalist', foreign art added weight to these demands in the realms of art and architecture. There were further limiting factors in the following years. Apart from looking back at avant-garde art of the twenties, it was primarily a keen, by no means uncritical, curiosity about contemporary Western art that helped the emergence of the 'inofficial' art that

304 Marina Lebedkina: light object, 1986. – 305 Andrei Andreiev: computer graphics composition using a photo by A Borissov, 1988.

306

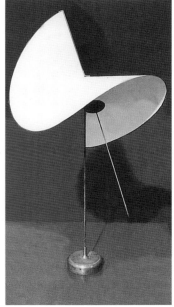

307

308

306 Irina Medvedeva: composition of folded paper, created during the Experimental Design Seminar at the VNIITE in Moscow, 1984. – 307 Mikhail Litvinov: model of a lamp with a paper lampshade, 1984. – 308 Work by participants of the Experimental Design Seminar at the VNIITE in Moscow, 1984.

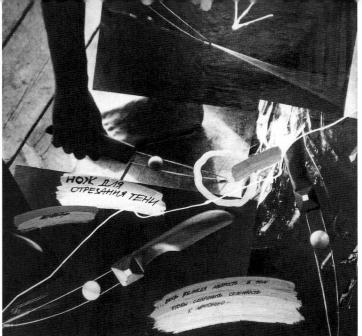

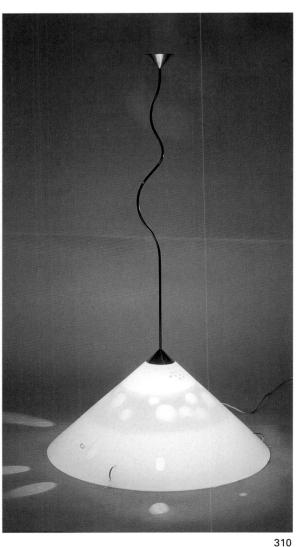

reached the public more and more in the period after 1975 (before this it had taken place in private circles). Exponents of what was still official Socialist Realist art were but little perturbed by these developments. This, in turn, did not hinder the experimental energy of young designers searching for new creative methods in the least. Their work reveals a great need to catch up. The spontaneous naivity, as well as imaginary, utopian, undisciplined and chaotic qualities of several designs can be seen as abruptly expressing a need for communication that has been blocked for a great length of time.

The kinetics expert and architect, Viatsheslav Koleitshak, embodied the 'scientific designer' for many of his contemporaries. Trying to teach and communicate, regarding the production of ideas as his primary function, his creations (mirror mobiles, optically broken constructions, sculptures made of ropes and poles) themselves would be enough to call the boundary between 'free' art and 'applied' design into question in a new manner. Of central importance are problems of spatial perception, taking into account the methods of Op-art. In 1993, he exhibited objects reminiscent of stage costumes and imaginary musical instruments.

309 Semion Krupin: *A Knife to cut away the Shadows,* metaphysical project, 1990. – 310 Irina Presnetsova: floor lighting with rotating sheet, 1986.

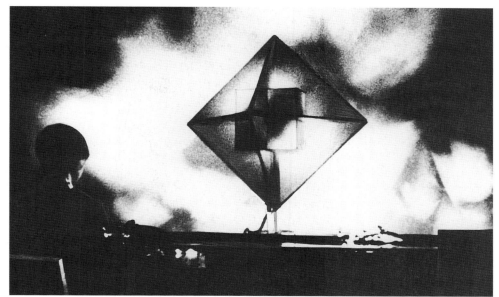

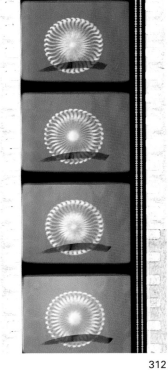

311 Prometheus Designer Studio in Kasan, (headed by Bulat Galeiev): light and music installation *The Crystal,* 1970s. – 312 Prometheus Designer Studio in Kasan (headed by Bulat Galeiev): stills from a mutimedia film with music by G Svidridov, 1970s. – 313 Alexander Lavrentiev: table lamp *The House of Colour Slides,* 1987.

314

315

There is no doubt that these objects have little in common with the functional aesthetics of furniture and everyday objects. They are visions, visual products, revealing the inner world of an obviously multi-faceted artist. Although his formal games do not reach the banal world of the consumer – at least not in their entirety – this does not exclude influence on young designers in a pedagogic and inspirational manner.

This is even more the case with experiments that took place at the Institute for Technological Aesthetics (VNIITE) in Moscow and seminars at the Design Centre. These events (within the general 'Experimental Design' category) had pedagogical and demonstration aims and were suitable for creating contacts and exchanging ideas. Some of the collectively created projects provided answers to stylistic phenomena of Western art (from Pop Art and computer art to Postmodernism) from the designer's point of view. An exhibition took place at the end of each seminar. The methodological framework, developed by V Vinogradov, I Presnetsova, A Chauke and designers from the furniture industry, inspired self-sufficient experiments and the construction of paper design models. Forms do not only consist of connected areas and constructive elements, they also characterise the object's function and have a certain metaphoric value. At the same time, attention was given to emotional perceptions and the release of associations. A chair, for example, gives the impression of being pleasantly warm. Another chair, where there is an interchange of smooth, soft and fixed areas, invites you to swing in it.

316

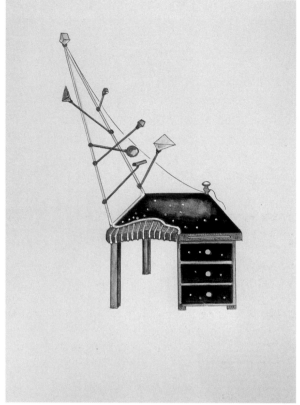

317

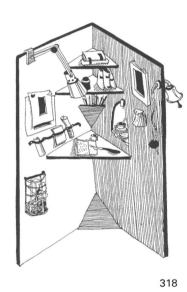

318

314 Tatiana Shulika: design for writing equipment with pen-holder, 1987. – 315 Alexander Ermolaiev: *The Window and The Chair*, objects made of synthetic materials, 1984.

316 Gennadi Vsorov: teapot, 1987. – 335 Yevgenia Poroshina: *The Concentrated Table*, 1987. – 317 and 318 Irina Presnetsova: *Emotional Furniture*, 1987. 319 Edas Studio of the Architectural School (headed by Vladislav Kirpitshev): Malevich Tower, made by students, 1980s.

Lighting and light kinetics play an important role in the work of VNIITE. Floor lighting was made from bent poles, lights containing matt or shining cones, with various openings in the form of elastic metal rings. A simple moving mechanism created highly aesthetic, rhythmic shadow and light effects on the walls. The graphic artist and textile designer, Alexander Pushkarev, concentrated on creating optical effects in textile ornaments. He teaches his students about photograms and collages, turning his back on stereotypical textile design. Patterns with obviously three-dimensional structures generate successful results.

Art education in Soviet schools was adequate to satisfy more than just average tastes for many years, as was the production of children's books and films. The level of even elementary classes, as regards diversity and methodology, was for the most part high. Apart from the schools, there was the Edas Studio, opened in Moscow in 1977, headed by Vladislav Kirpitshev. Here, children between the ages of six and fifteen were taught about the possibilities afforded by design. They learnt the basics of drawing, painting, three-dimensional design, modelling and simple architectural design. Great demands were made on the imaginative and creative craft abilities of the children by giving them interpretative and practical tasks which involved the creation of cardboard or paper models during a specific period of time.

Kirpitshev, who calls his method 'dynamic', is only one amongst many art educators who have realised that teaching visual creativity

319

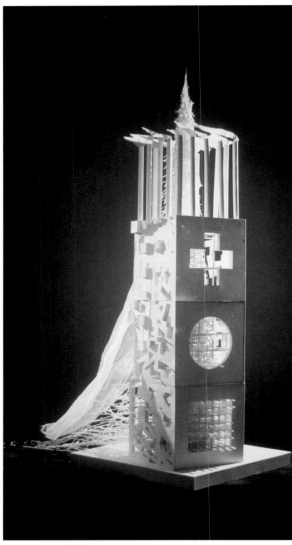

320

and the laws of harmony should commence during childhood, independent of material circumstances, social pressures and fashionable trends (alongside the teaching of other basic values important for human existence). Creativity can only flourish successfully in this manner.

320 Edas Studio of the Architectural school (headed by Vladislav Kirpitshev): composition, made by school children, 1980s.

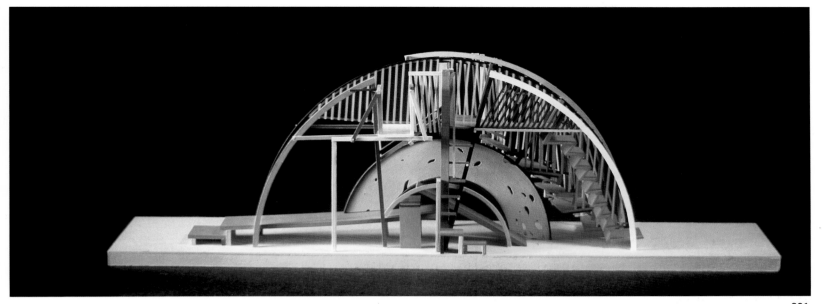

321

322

321 and 322 Edas Studio of the
Architectural School (headed by
Vladislav Kirpitshev): spatial
compositions, made from basic
architectural elements, made by
students, 1980s.

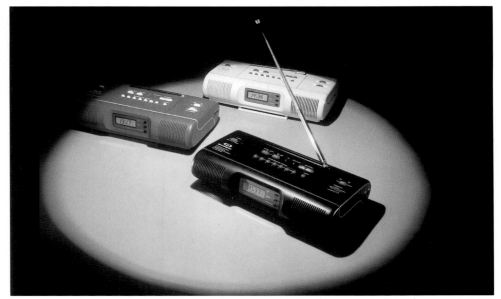

324

Problems of Emancipation

Design is not a profession but a part of human nature.
D Asrikan

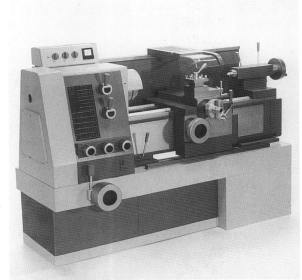

325

The social climate of the former Soviet Union was profoundly changed by increased economic cooperation with foreign states in the second half of the seventies, the advancement of Mikhail Gorbachev to General Secretary of the Communist Party in 1985 and the economic reforms commencing in the following year after the announcement of the 12th Five-Year-Plan in the spirit of glasnost and perestroika. The union was dissolved in 1991, eleven of the Republics forming the CIS (Community of Independent States) after the Baltic countries, White Russia, the Ukraine and other former Soviet Republics had declared their independence. With the collapse of State power, social structures, ways of thinking and acting changed, without what could be termed as a general, deep-seated democratisation of public life. Disorientation and helplessness were on the increase and the struggles of everyday life appeared to greatly contradict any reforms.

326

323 Shota Dsneladse: toy, 1988.

324 Vladimir Finogenov: transistors, 1990. Photo: V Kulkov. – 325 W Prochorov, A Grashin and others: universal bench, 1989. – 326 W Akopov, M Anikst and others: logo of the Promo Company, 1981.

Nonetheless, numerous small and medium companies were founded as private enterprises during the eighties (in the sphere of big industry, still in State hands). They followed the laws of free enterprise according to the laws of free enterprise. They were inspired by foreign products or attempted to imitate them

327

328

329

330

in such a way that at least the exterior of original and copy could hardly be distinguished
(interpreting copyright in a rather generous
manner). As private enterprise was revived, a
new era of Russian design appeared to be
dawning. The designs, however, were not always Russian in origin. Imitations replaced
originality, everyday gadgets after Western or
Far Eastern models giving an impression of
modernity, not based on any local traditions.
This hardly bothered consumers. Apart from
price, they were mainly interested in the
wealth of choice in comparison to earlier
times and, in certain cases, the practical,
everyday usefulness of a product in comparison to others.

A new business law gave companies more
autonomy in the summer of 1987. The State
system of taxes and controls became less
strict. Competence and personal initiative was
to replace the right to make decisions collectively. A flexible approach to the market was
to take precedence over a blind fulfilling of
plans. Increasing liberalisation of culture enabled the cessation of censorship, the growth
of an unusually large number of exhibitions
and the opening of depots where the musems
had banned a great many masterpieces of early Russian modernism, despite the meanwhile
worldwide fame of their creators. Contemporary Russian artists reacted in diverse ways to
the rich legacy of their country's avant-garde
(coming to the fore more and more) but, on
the whole, the lifting of restrictions concerning this was like a liberation that had been
overdue for a long time.

Due to new legislation, designers had the opportunity of either working for the State or as
freelance artists. It was now easy to exchange
textbooks, catalogues and other printed material with foreign colleagues; travel to congres-
ses in Japan, Europe and America; and take
up contacts with Western firms. Large exhibitions organised by the Committee for Science and Technology of the USSR showed the
latest industrial styles and technology from
other parts of the world. While a show limited
to the county of North Rhine-Westphalia was
more regional in character, the exhibition presented by the Stuttgart Design Centre and the
Industrial Reform House in Essen showed
what was new in West German design. The
'Design in the USA' exhibition and a special
presentation, entitled 'Tradition and Innovation', showing all aspects of Japanese ap-

plied arts, based on thousand-year-old traditions (and being wonderfully simple in
character) were particularly popular.

Such events, as well as foreign travel and pe-
rusal of Western textbooks in this perestroika
era, provided Russian artists and designers
with possibilities for comparison and initially
led to a sober appraisal of the situation at
home. This was probably due to confidence in
being able to keep up with the rapid technological developments in other industrialised na-
tions. This optimism was strengthened by
confidence in their own creativity which had
emerged in recent years, despite all material
and ideological obstacles. This was directed
more at solving local problems than at showing muscle in international competitions. As
far as could be seen, these problems were
numerous.

Attempts at founding an independent design
council were made within the VNIITE in the
mid-eighties, on the initiative of Yuri Soloviev.
No independent professional organisation
had existed until then. Designers had formerly
turned to the Artists' or Architects' Council in
order to receive confirmation of their status.
Becoming a member had guaranteed work
and social security, as well as some privileges
including the relatively cheap working conditions in rented design studios and State
workshops.

At this time, the creation of new professional
organisations was an arduous, bureaucratic
process, dependent on patience, dexterity and
good contacts. Prescribed channels were
highly complicated, leading from ministerial
cultural departments right to the Central Committee of the USSR. Soloviev managed to
bring about a positive decision, thanks to
connections in high Party and government
circles. Organisational problems, however,
that increased as the founding congress of
1987 drew nearer, demanded a great deal of
energy. In the meantime there were several
thousand designers in the former Soviet
Union, working in the most diverse industries
and, within these, in many different spheres.
The council was originally meant to unite
specialists from all areas of design. Textile designers, graphic artists and product designers
from various industries; scientists and educators, who specialised in design in some form
or fashion, were also considered.

327 W Charkov: type 17A
20PF40-4 universal bench which
can be programmed electrically,
switchboard can be adjusted
freely, 1990. – 328 Victor Charkov: coffee-machine for restau-
rant, 1989. Photo: W Kulkov. –
329 Nicolai Usoltsov, Nicolai
Kusnetsov: underground train
with driver's area, manufactured
by the Mytistchi Factory,
1991–92. – 330 V Obuchov, N
Kusnetsov and others: interior of
an underground compartment,
1991–92.

The founding committee sent news and questionnaires to all ministries and unions in order to register future members as smoothly as possible. The delegates were chosen according to the results of inquiries while a resolution of the Party Central Committee confirmed the oncoming foundation of the design council. Finally, on April 3, 1987, the founding of the Design Council took place in the Hall of Columns in the Council building in the centre of Moscow (there were 610 delegates from the entire Soviet Union). This was both the first and last federal congress before the Soviet Union was dissolved in favour of sovereign states. It was official and 'stately' in character, due to the presence of government officials, while the atmosphere of the founding and the mood of the participants was visibly dampened by the unusually democratic methods of procedure. More than 90 delegates were voted into the chief committee, each with the task of heading a specific part of the Council's activities. Amongst these was Soloviev, who had already been present during preparations.

Legislation passed in 1987, concerning the development of design in the USSR, did not, for the most part, come into effect, the main points dealing with goverment rights and finances. The goverment declined to finance the Design Council with State money (which was not the case with professional bodies already in existence). The suggestion that a part of company profits would go to the Council met with deaf ears although it was correctly argued that effective design had positive effects on the economic success of the product and therefore also on profitability.

The aforementioned, new industrial legislation hindered such contributions. Companies were now able to take control of profits independently. Legislation had therefore taken away the State's right to interfere in such decisions.

The new Design Council, however, was exempted from all taxation, including import, export and tax on profits. It was given a location in the centre of Moscow with low rent. The 1.2 million roubles provided as initial help, however, was modest in comparison with 9 million per annum given to the Artists' Council by the government and the 'purchases' of the Architectural Council, whereby each member donated seven per cent of his income. The increase in freedom, however, was of far greater importance, even if this could not be measured in numbers. Designers could now organise their offices and studios with official sanction. Dmitri Asrikan, a well-known designer, who had worked at the VNIITE with Soloviev for years, was amongst the first.

Events similar to the founding congress took part in other areas, as well as in other republics (in St Petersburg, Ekaterinburg, Samar, Volgograd, Togliatti and Nishni Novgorod). Several smaller and regional councils were formed and even the Moscow designers came together. The large umbrella organisation threatened to break apart into numerous groups, each with its own direction. During this process, Russian designers displayed a certain amount of decisiveness and stubborness in protecting their own rights. Finally, in April 1989, the Moscow Council was brought into being, more than two-and-a-half years before the Russian Design Council was founded (then in the heartland of the former Soviet Union).

Hope for industrial development went hand in hand with the passing of further legislation to help the emergence of private enterprise. There were enough grounds for such hope, despite unsuccessful State investment, the desolation of many companies, obvious mismanagement and the ever mighty mechanisms of a planned economy. The reforms, however, could not take effect in a matter of months. It took time before about ten new design studios had established themselves in Moscow and other Russian cities, able to survive by other means than contracts from flourishing private companies, as they were themselves private enterprises, founded by well known designers. Increasingly, State companies gave the sudios work, after discovering inland market possibilities and export opportunities.

331

A meeting of local and regional representatives in St Petersburg in 1989 initiated the founding of a design council limited to Russia alone. The necessary preliminary work was carried out by a provisional organisational committee. Internal political conflicts and general uncertainty about the outcome of the power struggle between Gorbachev and his rival, Boris Yeltsin, played a role in the fact that this took over two years. A plea to create the new council was made at a place near Minsk in October 1991. A short time later, representatives of individual Russian organisations met in Moscow in order to decide upon common rules. A horizontal, rather than traditional structure was envisaged. At the first meeting of the Russian Design Council in mid-1992, in Nishni Novgorod, Yuri Nasarov, a well-known designer, was voted in as president.

The developments that went hand-in-hand with political events also mirrored their contradictory elements. After the East-West conflict had been overcome, these reflected a search for a new national and social identity, the wish to leave behind old ideals and power structures and, even if not always visible to outsiders, the tensions between conservatives and liberals, as well as between orthodox and progressive, modern forces. Put simply, the process of renewal was similar to that which had taken place before the eyes of the world

332

331 W Esakov: model of an electric car, 1987. Photo: W Kulkov. – 332 W Karpovitch: home trainer, 1986. Photo: W Kulkov.

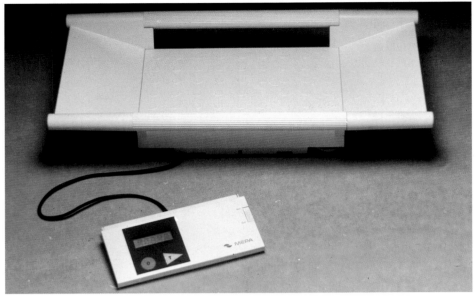

333

334

in 1917. This time, however, the constellations are more balanced, part of a multinational group of links, providing the willingness to cooperate with greater chances than the negative spirit of confrontation.

The teaching programmes at Russian design schools have been modernised to a certain degree in the last years. The Stroganov Art School in Moscow (specialising in industrial and graphic design) and the V I Muchin School for Industrial Art in St Petersburg, as well as the Architectural Institute in Ekaterinburg, are still the leading institutions. The Textile Academy in Moscow maintains its reputation as the most prestigious school for young textile and fashion designers.

The Moscow Architectural Institute has increasingly been recognised as an important design school in recent years. There, as is the case in St Petersburg, older teachers have continued to work with members of the middle generation and young assistants, leading to a high standard of teaching. Today it is hardly possible to ignore the experiences made by 'veterans' of design education – I Wax, A Korotkevitch, G Minervin, A Kvasov, S Neimand, V Surinei, V Shimko, T Koslvei. Their methods were linked to practical work and set new teaching standards for following generations of teachers – such well-known teachers as F Lvovski, A Ermolaiev, V Musichenko, J Grabovenko and V Muraviev. Exercises with personal computers help students to solve more complex problems. A large number of diploma projects, created at the end of the course, are challenging and original.

333 Sergei Ratnikov: scales which won a prize at the *Design '93* Competition in Moscow, 1993. Photo: W Kulkov. – 334 S Salski: child's *Bee* bicycle with spade, rake and bucket 1987.

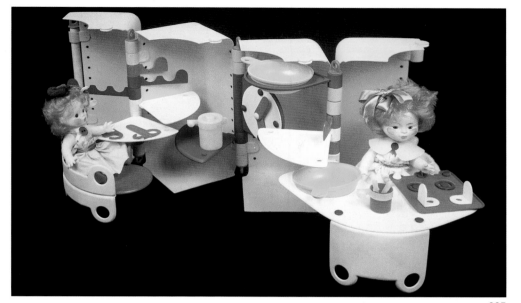

335

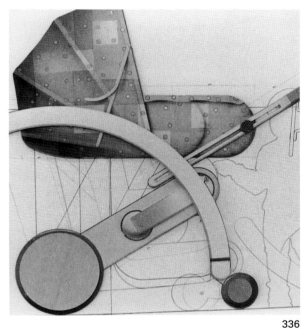

336

337

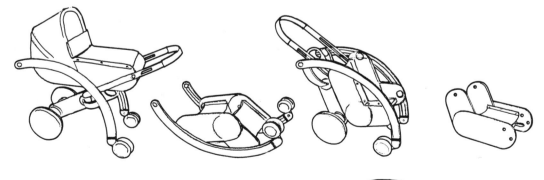

335 Foldable doll's house made of synthetic material, diploma at the Stroganov Institute of Decorative Arts in Moscow, 1980s. – 336 and 338 G Bodrikov: pram that can be folded in several ways, diploma at the Stroganov Institute of Decorative Arts in Moscow, 1993. – 337 Adolf Neistadt: wooden toy, 1988–89.

338

Student competitions, organised by the Design Council on a regular basis since 1988, contributed greatly to the encouragement of design education. The two most recent competitions, in St Petersburg in 1992 and Moscow in 1993, revealed a high standard of work, as well as a broadening of the network to other parts of Russia. It was difficult to establish new design faculties in cities such as Nishni Novgorod, Rostov on the Don, Kasan and Togliatti, mainly due to a lack of appropriate educational experience. The new design departments were initially headed by graduates of schools for applied arts in Moscow and St Petersburg, supported by working designers, architects and teachers at local construction institutes. It took time before the teaching staff included graduates of the new faculties or professionals from other regions. The dissolving of the USSR and the formation of sovereign states often led to the return of architects, engineers and designers who had worked outside Russia, in the Northern Caucasus or in the Central Asian Republics, for example.

Another educational trend is found in the art schools that are controlled by the Cultural Ministry of the Russian Federations and are part of local cultural administration. The Ivanovsky Art School in Moscow, whose programme was greatly influenced by Alexei Vedeneiev, is an example. The designers who studied here either completed further education at larger institutes or started working straight after their final exams. Exhibitions showing work by Russian art school graduates, organised once or twice a year by the Ministry of Culture, offered opportunities for comparison. The Design Council of Russia took part in one in 1993. Problems of design education on various levels, professional opportunities for graduates and possibilities for specialisation were discussed at length.

339

340

A committee deals with the coordination of teaching methods in 'higher' design education, consisting of representatives from all institutions with their own design faculties. Delegates from the Design Council of Russia belong to this, as well as to a council linked to the Ministry of Culture, concerned with aspects of teaching. In recent years, interest in alternative design education, such as that provided by private institutes, has grown. The first Design College was founded in Ekaterinburg, in cooperation with the Design Council and L Plyshevski, a professor at the local architectural institute. N Bogatova, a graduate of the Institute for Decorative Arts in Moscow (MCHPI), heads the design department at the College for Contemporary Art in Moscow. The roots of these purely state institutes reach back to the seventies when Vladislav Kirpitshev founded his Edas School for children of all ages. The new Moscow teaching studio, Start, under the patronage of the Architectural Council, follows his example. The teaching methods of the Children's Design Centre in the city of Orsk at the southern edge of the Urals, headed by Svetlana Sacharova, follow the example of the Youth Design School, founded in the eighties in St Petersburg by Sergei Talankin. Personal commitment and a great deal of idealism are important for educational success in all cases.

The same applies to numerous other bodies. They provide fresh ideas for art education in public schools and encourage the broadening of aesthetic consciousness, open to alternative and experimental forms of design (apart from adult educational programmes). There is not yet an organisation that gathers together all art and design schools that were founded privately. The Design Council of Russia, however, holds regular seminars to discuss methods and organises exhibitions for children's and youth studios.

341

342

339 W Vladimirov, I Sheliagin: walkie-talkies, 1989. Photo: W Kulkov. – 340 Dmitri Asrikan, O Voltshenkov: Kriket mini-tractor, 1990.

341 Gennadi Syshenko: driver's cabin for tractors, 1988. – 342 Protective working clothing, diploma at the Stroganov Institute of Decorative Arts in Moscow, 1980s.

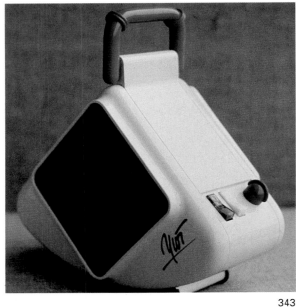

343

Contemporary Trends

It is rather difficult, if not impossible, to find unity in the stylistic tendencies of Russian design of the last ten to twelve years. It is also difficult to make judgements about these. The picture is changing constantly and all attempts at being objective and analysing it are made difficult by two factors. Firstly, quality designs fail, due to production conditions. Secondly, products after designs incorporating original ideas, are often uncompetitive in the international market, sometimes completely so. Many designs remain in the planning stage or are replaced by similar products with better technical means. In both cases, the design fails to be profitable without really even contributing towards this.

The market breakdown in Eastern Europe has made this situation even more difficult. After the disbanding of the Council for Mutual Economic Aid (1991), the economic ties between the former Socialist Democracies are subject to regulatory free market laws (products are put on offer and then chosen). Good product design can therefore only compete if it really is 'good' – as superior as possible and contributing to the overall achievement potential of the product. It is difficult to sell a beautiful and functional piece of furniture, made of impermanent and badly fabricated material, even if created by an eminent designer.

It is therefore the quality of industrially produced everyday products, rather than contemporary Russian design standards, that is

344

345

346

347

343 Tatiana Samoilova: electrical heater, 1980s. – 344 Tatiana Samoilova: quartz watches, part of the Watches Design Project, 1986. – 345 Tatiana Samoilova: pocket calculator, 1986. – 346 Tatiana Samoilova: hand sewing-machine, 1988.

347 Viatsheslav Stolnikov, Svetlana Usova: *Crossbill* and *Lizard* table lamps, 1987–88. – 348 N Getmanov, A Makarov: didactic toy, 1990.

348

349

problematic. Engineers can obtain Western 'know-how' more easily but this does not necessarily facilitate matters. A new spirit has long since been felt on a cultural level in art, theatre, film and architecture, without leaving behind certain traditions. Russian industry, however, had difficulties in developing technology further, as well as in impoving old products and creating new ones – although the demand for consumer items is actually growing, despite less buying potential and government subvention. Design often has an ambiguous role in this precarious economic situation.

This has played a part in the return of several designers to their original spheres of activity such as architecture, painting or graphic art. Others used the new, liberal emigration laws to go abroad (including Israel). The generation of designers trained after the last war has now disappeared. However, despite contemporary economic difficulties, their creative power lives on, linked to a hope for a better future and the successes of several private design studios and admiration their work receives abroad.

350

349 Vladimir Finogenov: compact stereo, 1991. – 350 V Kovshar: coin telephone, 1988.

351

Dmitri Asrikan's Moscow studio is undoubtedly the most well known studio that exists beyond the bounds of the Design Council. Asrikan had gathered together a group of talented people, including M Mikheieva, A Senelnikov and I Tarachkov. Each project was a modern alternative to traditional design, whereby the product was almost of secondary importance (a small ice-cream machine, a hairdryer with interchangeable parts, a heavy tractor). Technical elements, otherwise developed by engineers, are integrated optimally and can be used immediately; and forms have harmonious stylistic elements (following a worldwide trend). In this case again, creating greater quantities of the designs failed, due to technology problems. The models belong to the broad 'Work for its own sake' category or can be described as 'projects about the law of free falling' (as was stated by one of Asrikan's coworkers).

The Asrikan Studio's international reputation brought with it the possibility of taking part in competitions. The designs for a new underground train and a small bus received inland rewards. The GALO/BEN company was ac-

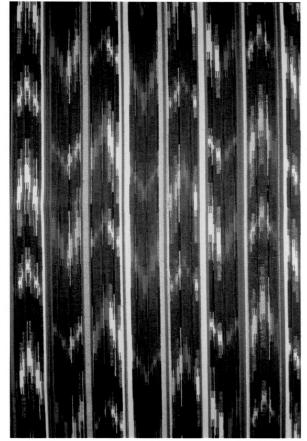

352

351 Irina Krutikova: *Birds,* fur coat, 1991. This won a fashion design prize from the Moscow City Council in 1992. – 352 Nina Datskovskaia: material design, 1987.

353

claimed for the designs of office furniture that 'makes use of new technologies'. At a competition in Japan in 1992, they received a prize for the model of a 'flying garden'. The most recent success was the creation of systems of visual communication for a concert in Moscow. Asrikan and his team regard their studio as a collective school. Each person learns from the others, younger members from their elders and vice versa, although they remain open to influences and inspiration from outside.

The School for Applied Arts in St Petersburg (S-PVCHPU) has had a special place amongst Russian art schools in the last ten to fifteen years. Students of the founder of the Department of Industrial Design, I Wax, have important positions there. In their work, they search for bridges between artistic traditions and modern technology and have created highly 'classical' forms. Tatiana Samoilova, who studied with Wax from 1956-58, mainly designed mass-produced consumer goods. She regards the diversity of the items as being condusive to her creativity – 'what is most important to me is a broad field of specialisation, searching for the new, love of colour and forms'. She attempts to hide the banal, everyday quality of such objects with new contours and materials, according to the latest style, without losing sight of functional aspects (whether dealing with lamps, simple wooden handles, massage machines, manicure sets, watches or razors). Samoilova herself cannot be blamed for the relatively low level of design production. Like many of her colleagues, she felt obliged to combine her ideas

354

355

353 Alexei Kolotushkin: *Kompressor,* 1989. Photo: W Kulkov. – 354 Yevgeni Lobanov and others: *Gnom* mini-car, maximum speed 120 km/h. – 355 Central Design Office for Farming Equipment (Rudolph Fedosov, Gennadi Petrov and others): 133 *Super* mowing-machine, 1987.

356

↑ 357

with old-fashioned technology and merciless, mercantile forces. She now heads one of the first private studios in St Petersburg, under the patronage of the Russian Design Council (and has taken part in design seminars in Norway, Armenia, Japan and the USA).

Andrei Meshtshaninov, another student of I Wax, worked with Tatiana Samoilova in the St Petersburg branch of the VNIITE, before opening his own studio in the city. He has a clear, rational style (whether for underwater machinery for divers, halogen lamps, medical first aid instruments or company logos). One of Meshtshaninov's most recent projects is developing design programmes for express trains on the Moscow-St Petersburg route.

The 'styling' of the compartments produced in the Togliatti city on the Volga for more than twenty years demonstrates how difficult it is to free oneself of aesthetic criteria, above all, when these are combined with certain technological standards. The huge company, created with the help of the Italian Fiat Company, built the popular Fiat 124 under licence, with the trade name Togliatti, after a famous Italian politician. This was sold both in Eastern European countries, as the Lada, and, having been developed further, widely in Western Europe. The Fiat, considered highly modern at first, was modified by Russian specialists after several years, so that the 'actual look' of the car could still be recognised although the models were changed and developed. The first major change was made by a graduate of the Design School in former Leningrad, Mark Demidovchev. The cross-country car Lada Niva, still

356 Evgeni Smirnov: glass bird scuplture, 1990. – 357 Elena Sudarushkina: female clothing in the 'Russian style', 1980s. – 358 Tatiana Suslova: *Dasha* kitchen for handicapped people, 1984–85.

358

ASSOCIATION

XXI

CENTURY

359

manufactured today, and the various models of family cars from Togliatti (with new bodywork and interiors) have visibly enriched Russian car design. On the other hand, even details complied with rather conservative taste. Robust dependability was considered more important than streamlined elegance.

Mark Demidovchev also played an important role in founding a regional design council in Togliatti ('Volgadesign'). Amongst the designs created here are plans and models for an underground train, where the designers N Usoltsev and N Kusnetsov made use of their experience in designing car interiors. Several smaller cars, like 'Oka', needing only little petrol and suitable for city traffic, were designed by council members, the first by J Vereshtshagin. The car was immediately popular amongst consumers, due to its successful bodywork and economical two-cylinder engine. The next model, Gnom, was designed by Evgeni Lobanov. In this case the streamlined form was the dominating element, slightly reminiscent of the forties and fifties and, at the same time, considered progressive. The recently opened, large scientific, technical automobile centre in Togliatti gives great hope for the future and could play a decisive role in increasing worldwide sales of Russian cars in the next years.

The basic rule – attractive design concepts that reveal their qualities when given concrete forms and judging these forms before a final decision is made about the design – has become a truism in artistic and industrial design, and was called into question by Russian

360

361

362

359 Leonid Feigin: logo for a social group, 1991. – 360 Vladimir Tchaika: cover of the periodical *Advertising*. The writing, imitating the Coca-Cola sign, reads 'No beer', 1990. – 361 Sergei Bobylev, Vladimir Kritshevski: cover pages of a schoolbook by E Upenski, 1990.

362 Victor Litvinov: installation at the Auto-Plakat Exhibition, 1988. – 363 and 364 Leonid Seniavski: model of the entrance to the Step Logic Company, beside it the company logo, 1993, a prizewinner at the *Design '93* Competition in Moscow. – 365 Victor Jakovlev: logo of the Aina Company, 1990. – 366 Leonid Seniavski: logo of the *Uspech* (Success) Company using Cyrillic and Latin letters, 1992.

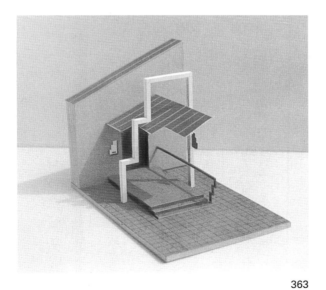

363

364

366

365

367

'paper design' in the seventies (as well as by Constructivist architectural utopias). Such drawings and models, whether created for teaching and learning or completely 'freely', made no attempts at permanence. This is also the case with a large number of more recent creations, whereby a much larger number deserve to be realised although this will not be possible. It is therefore only natural to tend to describe the designer's intentions as ideas, experiments, sketches, studies or suchlike, if designs cannot be realised, for whatever reasons. It is often a great achievement for these designs to take part in competitions or to gain public attention at exhibitions. On the other hand, experience has shown that events that give designs a certain aura of exclusivity do not necessarily encourage the sober calculations of the manufacturer. During the era of the Socialist planned economy, such problems hardly ever cropped up (and if they did, this was only peripheral).

Furniture design and the furniture industry are now rather like two rival brothers who nonetheless depend on one another. There is a lack of educational possibility in the case of the former and problems with technology in the latter. Wood is still the favourite material, whereby long craft traditions in furniture manufacturing are being continued. Yuri Slutshevski, who has trained generations of furniture designers, is an outstanding specialist in this field, known all over the country. Alongside the schools for industrial design in St Petersburg and Moscow, there is another important educational centre for furniture design in Moscow which emerged from the Rus-

368

367 Yuri Slutshevski: armchairs, triptych, 1989. – 368 Dmitri Asrikan: television with stereo loudspeakers, 1991. Photo: V Kulkov.

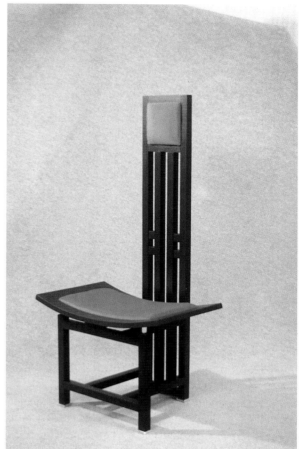

370

369

369 Alexander Igmant: male clothing, 1991. – 370 A Teterin: chair, 1990. – 371 Tamara Tsvetkova: mechanical clock, diploma at the Stroganov Institute of Decorative Arts in Moscow, 1993.

371

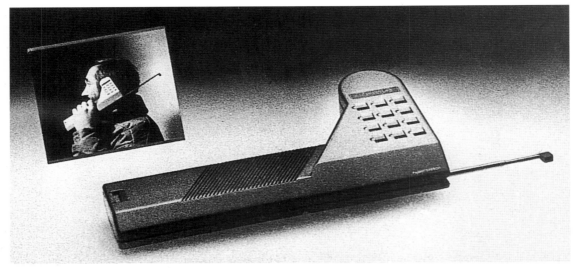

372

373

sian Institute for Furniture Design and Technology. Foam and synthetic material for covers are increasingly replacing traditional materials for filling and covering furniture, without greatly contributing to functionality, comfort and aesthetic qualities. Therefore, light steel constructions in chairs appear all the more pleasant. Aluminium is being increasingly used (alongside traditional wood) for the frames of chairs, armchairs and stools. The atmosphere of offices therefore acquires a pleasant dose of functionality, with such consciously sober mass-produced furniture, without allowing anonymity to pervade. The transition from heavy, representative furniture to light pieces, constructed according to ergonomic principles, is a slow process. Here, as is the case in other fields, old habits die hard and new developments are impeded, even if they are obviously better.

Taking the furniture of an average Russian apartment in a metropolitan slab construction into account, the enormity of the Russian designer's task becomes apparent, above all for the furniture designers who wish to

372 Andrei Taube: cordless telephone, 1989. – 373 Sergei Leonov, Nord Design Studio: table lamp with dimmer, 1989.

374

375

remain faithful to their professional ethos as creators of style and taste. It is difficult to replace stereotypical decorating styles with furniture appropriate for individual needs without a great deal of persuasion and this cannot be instigated by schools alone. This is made more difficult by a dearth of apartments and the power of habit – a tendency to be complacent that is part of the Russian character. With this social background, made even more complex by the present economic crisis, new Russian furniture designs appear like harbingers of a rosier future. Examples could be seen at the Grand Palais in Paris in February 1990. Monumental seating ensembles, created after designs by Slutshevski, harmonised with chairs and armchairs, designed by some of his students. Sometimes avantgarde, formal solutions were united with fine, light, ironic humour, reminiscent of the time before perestroika. The young designer, I Dimitriev, attempted to demonstrate the Russian conception of the term 'postmodern' in his 'Circus' chairs, using ideas from Russian turn-of-the-century artists such as Viktor Vasnetsov and Mikhail Vrubel. A Teterin's chair was inspired by the timelessly beautiful furniture designs by the architect, Charles Rennie Mackintosh. A Smagin, who delights in confusing the public with his designs, created a stir with a 'chair' that makes fun of the idea of chairs in general. It is highly elegant, combining metal tubes with tiles.

An exhibition of all designs that had been in a Russian competition, organised by the Design Council and the Zentro Furniture Factory, took place in Moscow at the end of 1991. The standard, above all of the work from Moscow, was very high. A rather modest, balanced style took precedence over fashionable eccentricity and extravagence. Designs that were created jointly by furniture and textile designers were particularly successful. The result was that the chair and cushion covers

374 Oleg Shoka: interior of a living-room, 1988. – 375 Sergei Leonov: chandelier with *Zirkonia* prisms, 1989.

376

377

they produced offset the aesthetically formal qualities of the seating furniture to even greater advantage.

Book publications and large, popular exhibitions have also reawakened interest in Russian avant-garde art of the twenties outside the Soviet Union. This has helped the rediscovery of some of the most talented exponents of textile design of that time. Women such as Varvara Stepanova, Olga Rosanova and Liubov Popova, whose abstract textile designs revolutionised the ever re-occurring industrial textile designs, were admired as role models by their young successors. Additionally, there was greater knowledge of Russian textile art, which had developed as part of the peasant craft culture in the seventeenth century before being reproduced in factories. Young designers at the Institute for Decorative Arts in Moscow (MCHPI) and at the Faculty for Applied Decorative Art at the Textile Academy are taught a great deal about traditional methods of manufacturing, use of colour and printing methods as a basis for textile design.

378

Graduates from both institutions today greatly influence the style of textiles in Russia. Patterns and colour reproduction, created by printing machinery, as well as the way each material is made and structured, are examples of this influence. All these elements must be chosen according to aesthetic and technological points of view and are combined in an optimal manner. Successful experiments made in the field of spinning and colour techniques by designers Nina and Alexandra Datskovskaia lead to further experimentation. One

376 Alexander Gurevich: interior of a bedroom, *(The Rocker)*, 1990. – 377 Sergei Novikov: stereo radio, diploma at the Stroganov Institute of Decorative Arts, Moscow, 1993. – 378 I Saitsev: toy car with battery power, 1990.

379

379 Dmitri Asrikan: *Rapan* camper, 1989. – 380 Design department of the AZLK Moscvich Factory, Alexander Sorokin, Marat Yelbaiev and others: *Arbat* estate car, 1988.

380

381

383

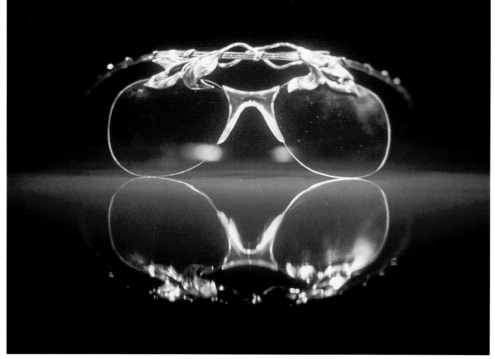

382

381 Dmitri Asrikan: experimental model of an underwater town *(Aqua),* 1987. – 382 Boris Bodrikov: spectacles, 1991. – 383 A Bedakov: automatic climate control, 1991.

384

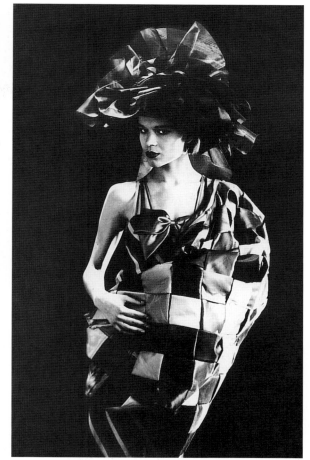

such experiment succeeded in dyeing linen in such a manner that it shimmers with all the colours of the rainbow, while tones change like a chameleon according to the light surrounding the viewer and the angle of viewing. Irina Vorobieva became known for her furniture and curtain material – her instinctive feeling for form is combined with artistic talent, whereby she designs textiles ideally suited for a certain area of an armchair or the seat and back of a chair.

Two friends, Alexander Soifer from Moscow and Sergei Shtoda from Piatigorsk, are leading contemporary carpet designers. While Soifer focuses on corresponding inter-relationships in his designs, taking note of architectural contexts including objects filling a living space, Shtoda concentrates entirely on colour effects of many nuances in his machine-woven carpets. His style avoids use of hard contrasts and asymmetry, concentrating instead on achieving extremely differentiated colours by using up to six shades of a primary colour. This painterly quality is allied with a high level of technical ability. Shtoda is more a 'classical' traditionalist than a stylistic or educational innovator.

In fashion, apart from imports from Western countries, the choice has become wider in recent years. Competition to win the attention of consumers has become more lively. The times when designers could solely create new items in State factories is now a thing of the past. Only the Design Council had a certain amount of freedom, as it kept up the tradition of theatrical costumes and exhibited the work

386

↑ 385

384 A Meshtshaninov: machine for professional divers, 1990. – 385 Dress model, 1990. – 386 W Netshaiev: dress model, 1990.

of young fashion designers from time to time. In contemporary Russian design it is necessary to differentiate between eccentric, extravagant creations trying to outdo one another with fairly bizarre ideas, and items that are sold as ordinary consumer goods, without losing chic or collecting dust on a shelf.

Viatsheslav Saitsev and Valentin Yudashkin can be counted amongst the 'stars' of contemporary Russian fashion design. Their playful designs appear to stem from a highly rich imaginative source. Irina Krutikova, who is similarly well known, uses her creative abilities more pragmatically. She trained in Berlin and has won numerous prizes. She uses her great sense of style mainly to design leather goods. The distinctive quality of her creations is a result of the manner in which she combines various types of fur, and of her elegant cuts.

Vladimir Netshaiev is a Russian fashion designer who has set up his own business. After working for larger fashion houses for several years, he founded a firm called Trans-Design. He enjoys using natural leather and light materials such as silk and synthetics, his creations revealing a preference for geometric forms, reminiscent of the twenties. The strengths of the Victoria-A trading company in Moscow, founded by Victoria Andrianova, and the Kollektsia, specialising in shoe design, are originality and quality. Privately founded and headed by Irina Selitskaia, their policy lies in the conscious rejection of mass-produced goods in favour of originality and quality.

The production of jewellery and accessories has increased so greatly that it is hard to keep track. Traditional hand-crafted production, involving only minor use of machinery, has once again gained popularity. Before the nineteenth century when machine production was introduced, a whole branch of Russian crafts specialised in making accessories. This took place in workshops, such as the one in Kasan, that had a high reputation, thanks to its great artistic merit. Part of this tradition is carried on in Sergei Leonov's studio in St Petersburg. The Zirkonium Company makes jewellery of

387

388

387 Shoe models, 1990. – 388 Interior of a living-room, 1988.

rare beauty, using the silver-grey metal of the same name, based on his designs.

Moscow designer Evgenia Vasilieva has specialised in designing suitcases, travel bags and handbags. She graduated from the Textile Academy and worked in a small leather factory. In 1989, she took part in a Soviet-American design seminar in Tibilissi. The originality of her designs helped her gain international success. Today, Vasilieva is an independent designer who runs her own workshop. Most of her work is sold to the United States. Several pieces from her latest collection were acquired by the Leather Museum in Offenbach.

It appears that general hopes for international recognition and cooperation are realised best in the successes of Russian fashion and costume design. Russian designs are becoming more apparent at fairs abroad because of their interesting ideas. Moreover, they have left behind their earlier air of conservatism which made them appear exotic in a strangely paradoxical manner to Western eyes. They seemed like messages from a distant, strange country that lay behind closed borders. Since the borders were opened and exhibitions have helped to create an adequate impression of the many facets of Russian fashion design, 'small suppliers' have started to seek popularity. One of these is Yuri Melnikov, a Moscow designer, who had a successful Berlin exhibition in 1991. His favourite combination of material is crumpled leather and metal. The accessories he has designed range from belts, bracelets and bags to artistically styled headgear.

Anatoli Kusmin creates fashion that is 'all of a piece'. His works are an arrangement in which each part contributes to the total impression. Kusmin, who initially worked as an independent artist, is now one of the most creative and individual members of his profession. He particularly enjoys working with materials such as German silver, mother-of-pearl and resin. As in the case of Vladimir Netshaiev, his preference for geometric patterns and assymmetrical compositions is reminiscent of the formal language of avant-garde Russian textile design in the twenties. This still remains, or has again become, a surprisingly rich source of inspiration for designers in search of a decorative style, appropriate for our time.

389

390

389 Anatoli Kusmin: jewellery, 1991. – 390 Alexander Smagin: twin chairs, 1989.

391

Challenges and Opportunities

It is difficult to make any prognoses about economic and social change that is taking place in Russia at present. It is impossible to foresee the time when there will be some degree of consolidation after the introduction of a market economy and the privatisation of State factories. Some areas of design are in a similarly uncertain condition. Sometimes the design market has qualities that are promotional and affect profitability, being an integral part of the product itself (most industrial products fall into this category), but it is unwise to make superficial judgements about this.

New and successful opportunities are appearing in industrial design, as a classical means of designing products. This does not seem to be diminished by the fact that foreign investors usually bring their own complete design programmes and even product forms and logos that are known all over the world, making the work of local designers superfluous or reducing it to a minimum. Possibilities for Russian design lie in original invention, linked to concrete market needs and a rejection of shortlived trends.

Unlike the sixties and seventies, when all larger industries had their own central design office, there are now only a few specialised designers working in industry. Most Russian designers reject such one-sided tasks. Many complain about the lack of interesting contracts and the lack of support from industrial leaders. Those who have remained, however, form a mainstay of the profession.

Amongst these is Tagir Chairov who teaches at the Faculty for Metalwork at the Moscow Institute of Decorative Arts (MCHPI). After working in a design office for several years, he became an assistant and then chief designer for farming machinery. He is presently setting up a large design office. The secret of his success rests upon the combination of three factors: rational methods of production, optimal usefulness that can keep up with high demands and an aesthetic design of exterior form. Some elements could be labelled as aerodynamic 'neo-baroque', consciously objective modernist in style, or ultra-modern high-tech that makes use of the latest technology. Chairov's credo is that each machine should be a 'visual revelation' that enriches the everyday with aesthetic qualities.

392

391 Alexander Smagin, Irina Vorobdoshova: sofabed 1990. – 392 Andrei Meshtshaninov: halogen lamp, 1992.

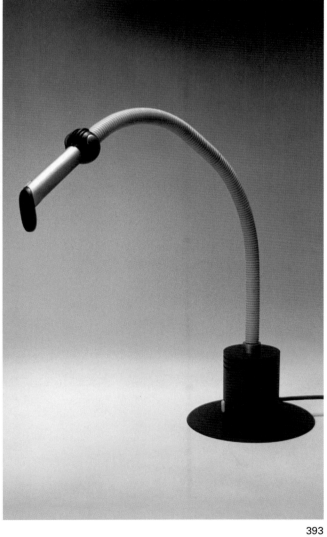

393

394

393 V Stolnikov, S Usova: halogen table lamp, 1990. – Vladimir Netshaiev: dress model,
1991, diploma at the Stroganov
Institute of Decorative Arts in
Moscow, 1993.

395

396

The industrial design product created when industrial design abilities are combined with knowledge of technology and materials, is given a dimension that breaks through its material confines. Mikhail Blok, a representative of the older generation who influences the work of W Kobylinski, J Dolmatovski and J Sumov, has an engineering degree, in addition to his other qualifications. This helps him to achieve highly creative feats in various areas, above all in developing small aeroplanes, a branch of Russian aeronautics that has been flourishing for some time. Blok's speciality is ergonomically ingenious arrangements of steering and control systems, suitable for small spaces.

Alongside Chairov and Blok, Vladimir Finogenov is the third important industrial designer with a great influence on education. Finogenov also trained as an engineer and has designed many types of microwaves, televisions and tape-recorders. Their subdued forms and colours appear somewhat 'academic'. They therefore appeal to a rather conservative taste, without being old-fashioned. Many of his numerous students and assistants, including V Vladimirov, S Ratnikov, I Sheliagin, A and P Teltevski, have become well-known designers themselves, each influencing the development of contemporary Russian industrial design in their own field.

Today, this development appears strangely halting since it is dependent on economic reform. This impression is strengthened by the

397

presence of so much creative potential. It seems that the real challenge for Russian design still lies ahead, after the battle between a planned and a market economy has been fought.

This could equally be the case with other areas of design that could widen the meaning of the traditional term. Many projects by Tatlin and El Lissitsky had similar effects in the twenties. There were also film and theatre designs, *street art* and a branch of architecture that defined industrial fairs, which later provided the framework for all kinds of exhibitions. This tradition, linked to work by Lissitsky, Konstantin Melnikov and the Vesnin architect brothers in the twenties and thirties, received fresh impetus in the sixties, a time in which the former Soviet Union wanted to gain international recognition for its industrial development. N Klix, K Roshdestvenski and N Grishin were known for their work as exhibition designers during this time.

Whereas obtrusive propaganda used to dominate exhibition styles, there is now a pleasantly pragmatic quality. Advertising has subverted ideology and according to theme and purpose, objectivity and a rejection of merely bombastic effects and competitiveness, combined with quality, have gained the upper hand. On the other hand, there have been fewer large, lucrative contracts in recent years. There are a number of young Russian designers who have specialised in exhibition design. These include L Peida, W Timofeiev, O Medvedev, O Lomako, as well as A and W Konorevy. In 1993, A Golyshev, J Diakonov and G Sinev received a prize for their new presentation of Russian works of art at the Tretiakov Gallery in Moscow.

Viktor Litvinov is one of the most eminent contemporary exhibition designers. He began as a member of a design collective and became the leading designer of a State economic collective. He was responsible for the design of numerous Soviet exhibitions at home and abroad. He writes about his many experiences in a book that analyses the work of Russian and foreign colleagues (*Setting Up Modern Exhibitions*). After being chief editor and publisher of a periodical for contemporary design, he founded his own business called Studio Quadrat in 1989. He has designed exhibitions in Mongolia, Germany, Italy, Hungary and Argentina for the Design Coun-

cil. Apart from this, Viktor Litvinov is known internationally for his extensive poster collection which he has exhibited in Moscow, Italy, the United States and Latin America with a great deal of success.

In the time of perestroika the poster has also regained its traditional function. For decades it was above all an ideological, political tool with stereotypical, reocurring slogans. Now it is being used by commercial advertising, without having to give up the artistic quality present in much graphic art in the thirties. This was confirmed by the 'Golden Bee Competition,' held in Moscow at the end of 1992.

Such well known contemporary Russian poster artists such as W Avakumov, I Maistrovski, I Beresovski, J Bokser and V Chaika were among the participants. The results of the competition revealed that all entries had great formal qualities. In recent years, the over-used appeal function of the poster, choking in its own pathos, has receded in favour of original company and product advertising.

Confronting artistic tradition does not necessarily imply mere imitation of its formal language. Instead of taking up ideas from the former avant-garde, contemporary Russian graphic designers attempt to learn from it, gain inspiration and take up a form of dialogue with it. Factory emblems or product trademarks have never completely disappeared and in recent years, emblems and logos of old and new corporations have flooded the country. Their colours enliven shop displays and advertising and flit across television screens.

The graphic design of periodicals has become more lively. An imposing example is Alexei Batshurin's periodical of popular science, *Snanie-Sila*. This was first presented at the Graphics Biennale in Bruno and has already become a 'classic' of modern typography and lay out. Vladimir Chaika's work for *Reklama* and *Greatis* also received a prize. *Greatis* received the Moscow Design Council Prize for its appealing and elegant presentation. Alexander Gelman designed several covers for *Technological Aesthetics* which has since been discontinued. He also received a prize for his highly sober style, strongly reminiscent of Constructivism. There are two new periodicals whose unconventional exterior guarantees a young readership. Alexandra Archutika

395 Alexei Fedotov: model of a cordless telephone with display and calculator, diploma at the Stroganov Institute of Decorative Arts in Moscow, 1993. – 396 Anatoli Senko: model of a skate-boarding rink, made of convertible parts, diploma at the Stroganov Institute of Decorative Arts in Moscow, 1993. – 397 Viatcheslav Glinin: *Carnival in Venice* table clock, diploma at the Stroganov Institute of Decorative Arts in Moscow, 1993.

398

399

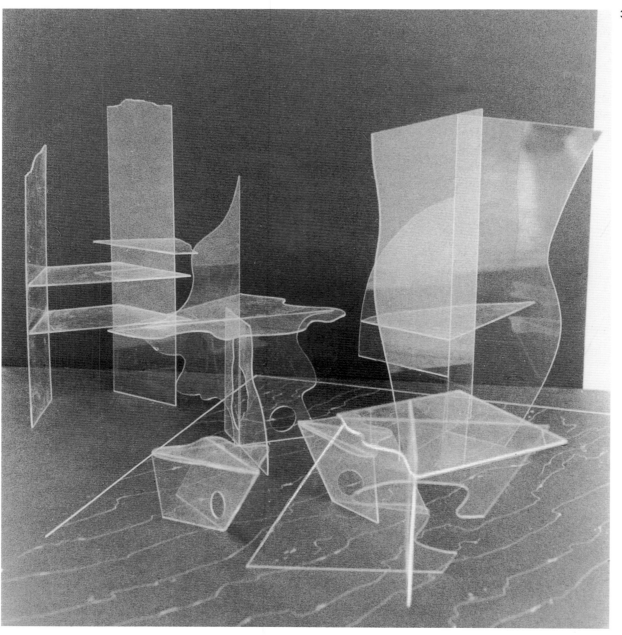

398 Arseni Soldau: television with exchangeable screens, diploma at the Stroganov Institute of Decorative Arts in Moscow, 1993. – 399 Ilia Pilstrov: transparent elements for exhibitions, diploma at the Stroganov Institute of Decorative Arts in Moscow, 1993.

is responsible for *hot-rocks* and Konstantin Kuchtin designs *Anons*.

Vladimir Chaika's work began to be exhibited as early as his student days. He is one of the most talented and uncompromising graphic designers of the middle generation who returned to design at the dawn of the Gorbachev era after several years of inactivity. He correctly and optimistically gauged the new possibilities opening for the most creative and stubborn talents in all areas of artistic life. Chaika embodies the successful designer with many contacts, thanks to his long-standing international reputation, who still suffers under the insufficiencies, provisional arrangements and, above all, uncertainties about the future in today's economic climate.

Chaika's frustrations are shared by numerous Russian colleagues who have contributed to the liberation of design in their country after a long period of anonymity. The young generation, in particular, realises that it is not sufficient to have one's own studio and make above-average artistic creations in order to remain in the profession and be successful internationally. It is useful to have knowledge of management and marketing, as well as experience with new technology. It is necessary to make use of the numerous contacts the Russian Design Council has made with State organisations, industry, educational institutions, private companies and professional bodies abroad.

The Russian Design Council has about 2,000 members, 800 of whom are in Moscow. The figures reveal an abstract potential, rather than giving information about concrete working conditions. They do not show the social and cultural influence of contemporary Russian design. They do, however, confirm two facts. Firstly, that there is a similar concentration of artistic activity in the capital which dominates other large cities, as was the case in the twenties. Secondly, that there is wide interest in the harmonisation of art and technology in a world that is growing more complicated and alienated from man with its remaining beauty.

List of Dates

1917 General strike in Petrograd, February Revolution, the Czar steps down. People's Commission for Education (NARKOMPROS) is founded in Petrograd, headed by A Lunacharsky. First issue of *Supremus,* edited by K Malevich, which becomes a forum for the Suprematists. October Revolution, Bolsheviks take over power, civil war breaks out.

1918 A Federal Russian Department for Visual Art (ISO NARKOMPROS) is created at the Governmental Commission for Education in Petrograd and Moscow, headed by D Shterenberg. First exhibition of the Moscow Association of Painters. An artists' union is founded in Petrograd, the Stroganov School of Art in Moscow is renamed the First Free Art Workshops, the Institute for Painting, Sculpture and Architecture is renamed as the Second Free State Art Workshops. The Museum for Visual Culture in Petrograd is founded. The First State Exhibition is opened in Moscow.

1919 Further art exhibitions in Moscow, parallel events in Petrograd and other Russian cities. ISO NARKOMPROS gives V Tatlin a contract to design a *Monument for the III International.* White Russia and the Ukraine declare themselves independent Soviet republics.

1920 Plan to provide the Soviet Union with electricity is drawn up. The UNOVIS association of artists is founded with branches and exhibitions in various cities. The Institute for Artistic Culture (INCHUK) is amalgamated with ISO NARKOMPROS in Moscow, Malevich, Rodchenko, El Lissitsky and Tatlin are members. The Manifesto of Realism is published by Naum Gabo, N Pevsner and G Klutsis in conjunction with their Moscow exhibition. The First and Second Free State Art Workshops are amalgamated to form the VCHUTEMAS (Higher Workshops of Art and Technology) in Moscow, Tatlin's model of a Monument for the *III International* is exhibited in Petrograd and is brought to Moscow in December. Russian artists participate in Venice Biennale. First Federal Russian Congress for Proletarian Culture *(proletkult).*

1921 Lenin visits the VCHUTEMAS in Moscow. The New Economic Policy (NEP) is declared at the 10th Party Congress of the Communist Party. 2nd Moscow exhibition of OBMOCHU (Society of Young Artists), founded in 1919, by Contructivists such as Rodchenko, Stepanova, the Stenberg brothers, A Gan and others. *5 x 5 = 25 Exhibition* in Moscow, with five works by five participants (Exter, Vesnin, Rodchenko, Stepanova, Popova). INCHUK decide to encourage *production art* despite protests by the Association of Easel Painters. Russian posters are exhibited in New York. Kronstadt Uprising after the supression of the democracy of Soviets is crushed by the Red Army.

1922 Metalwork Faculty opened at the VCHUTEMAS in Moscow. Association of Revolutionary Russian Artists (ACHRR) founded, promotes proletarian art. The Higher Institute of Art and Technology (VCHUTEIN) is founded in Petrograd (as a result of the amalgamation of the Free State Workshops and the Institute of Technical Drawing). Marc Chagall emigrates to Paris via Berlin. Kandinsky teaches at the Bauhaus in Weimar. El Lissitsky and Ilia Ehrenberg publish the *Vieshtch-Object-Objet* periodical in Berlin. First exhibition of Russian art in Berlin at the Van Diemen Gallery. Constructivists begin to work for the theatre (set and costume designs). Stalin becomes Secretary-General of the Party. 10th Federal Russian Congress decides to form the Union of Socialist Soviet Republics (USSR).

1923   The Futurist periodical LEF (Left Artists' Front) is founded by Mayakovsky and Ossip Brik. Malevich becomes Director of the State Institute for Artistic Culture (GINCHUK) in Petrograd. Mayakovsky and Rodchenko begin to work together in advertising. The first Federal Farm and Crafts Exhibition in Moscow with participation of avant-garde artists. The Association of New Architects (ASNOVA) is founded in Moscow with N Ladovsky, V Krinsky, A Echimov and other VCHUTEMAS graduates. Rodchenko's typographical work for publishers. The first Government of the USSR is formed under the leadership of Lenin.

1924   Lenin dies in Gorki and is succeeded by Stalin, L Kameniev and G Sinoviev as Party leaders. Travelling exhibition of Russian art in the USA. El Lissitsky designs the *Bridge over the Clouds Skyscraper* in Moscow. Manifesto of Constructivist Architecture by M Ginsburg. The first Discursive Exhibition opens in Moscow with participation of numerous avant-garde groups of artists. The Constructivist film *Aeliat* (G Protasanov) with designs by A Exter is made and premiered. Russian artists have their own section at the Venice Biennale. L Popova dies.

1925   The Exposition Internationale des Arts Décoratifs et Industriels Modernes is opened in Paris with a Soviet pavilion (designed by K Melnikov), the model of a workers' club by Rodchenko, works by Stepanova, Popova, A Vesnin, Kandinsky and others. The Association of Easel Artists (OST) is founded in Moscow to counteract production and abstract art. The Four Arts Group and the Association of Contemporary Artists (OSA), which emerged from the Left Art Front (LEF), are founded. Constructivist cinema posters are exhibited in Moscow. El Lissitsky returns to Russia. The 14th Party Congress is renamed as the Communist Party of the Soviet Union (Bolsheviki), new party statute.

1926   The *New Architecture* periodical, mouthpiece of the Constructivists, is founded. The second exhibition of Constructivist film posters and the Society of Easel Painters (OST) in Moscow. The experimental department of the GINCHUK (State Institute for Artistic Culture) in Leningrad is closed. The *Soviet Art* and *Soviet Photography* periodicals are founded. The VCHUTEMAS is reorganised and renamed as VCHUTEIN (Higher Institute of Arts) in 1927. Travelling exhibition of Soviet art in Japan. Kandinsky has a one-man show in Western Europe. First typographic work by V Stepanova.

1927   The Diamond-Jack Group exhibits in Moscow. Third exhibition of easel painters (OST). Soviet art is exhibited in Tokyo. Federal Farming Exhibition in Moscow with participation of Russian avant-garde artists such as El Lissitsky and D Shterenberg. The woodwork and metalwork faculties at the VCHUTEMAS-VCHUTEIN are amalgamated. commemorative exhibitions marking the 10th anniversary of the October Revolution in Western European capitals. 15th Party Congress of the Soviet Communist Party, excluding Trotsky and others. Decision to collectivise farming.

1928   The start of the first Five Year Plan (1928–32). El Lissitsky designs the Soviet Pavilion at the *International Pressa Exhibition* in Cologne. The October Group of Artists and Architects is founded in Moscow, the manifesto is published in *Pravda*. The *Novi Lef* periodical which had emerged from the LEF (Left Art Front) in 1927, and Soviet Art (after 1929 succeeded by *Iskusstvo*) are discontinued. The exhibition *Soviet Textiles for Daily Life* is opened in Moscow. Another exhibition compares modern French and Russian art.

1929   Exhibition of Soviet crafts (also for sale) in large American cities. First theatre design exhibition in Moscow. *Daiosh! (Forward!)*, the workers' periodical for art, literature and politics is discontinued. Malevich retrospective in Moscow. First exhibition of the Association of Moscow Costume Designers. Thematic exhibition about the life of Soviet children, with participation by important groups of artists. Founding of the VOPRA architectural association (Federal Association of Proletarian Architects), opposition to formalism and bourgeois trends in Soviet architecture. A Lunacharsky steps down as head of NARKOMPROS (Peoples' Commission for Cultural Education).

1930 The periodical *The Building Up Of The Soviet Union* is founded, also appearing in English, Italian and German until 1941. V Mayakovsky commits suicide. The October Association has an exhibition in Moscow with work by Rodchenko, Stepanova, El Lissitsky, Klutsis and others. The VCHUTEIN in Moscow is reorganised into separate institutes (architecture, printing, textiles), leading to the formation of a new structure; the faculties for painting and sculpture are transferred to Leningrad. Large exhibition of Soviet art in Vienna, Berlin, London and Stockholm. The train service Turkestan-Siberia is opened (2,160 kilometres).

1931 V Molotov is elected as head of the Council of Peoples' Commissioners. Announcement of the First Competition for the Soviet Palace Project. The OST (easel painters) Association is disbanded. The Anti-Imperialist Exhibition is held in the Central Cultural and Recreational Park in Moscow to celebrate the May 1st holiday; El Lissitsky is nominated as leading artist-architect of the permanent architectural exhibition. The Soviet Union participates in the International Book Art Exhibition in Paris. Tatlin receives the title Honourable Artist of the USSR.

1932 After previous attacks due to accusations of formalism, the Central Committee of the Communist Party decides to disband the ASNOVA, ARU and OSA architectural associations. The exhibition *Contemporary Art in the USSR* is shown in Chicago and New York. Mayakovsky exhibition at the Literature Museum in Moscow. Tatlin has a one-man show and demonstrates his Letatlin flying machine (designs and constructions since 1929) at the Fine Arts Museum in Moscow. Large jubilee exhibition 'Russian Artists of the Last Fifteen Years in Leningrad' with about 3,000 works. N Suetin becomes artistic director of the State Lomonosov Porcelain Facory.

1933 The commencement of the Second Five Year Plan (1933–37). Further implementation of the Decree to Restructure Artists' Associations (1932), groups and associations are disbanded, the first great wave of political, ideological repressions against artists suspected of formalism. Georgi Stenberg and Leonid Vesnin die.

1934 Competition to redesign the Red Square in Moscow with buildings for heavy industry, with contributions by A and V Vesnin, I Leonidov and K Melnikov. First flight of the agitatory Maxim Gorki aeroplane (ANI-20). Progress is made in industry and farming collectives. Increase of historicising trends in architecture and urban planning (Neo-Classicism). Stalin personality cult has an effect on visual art. First Soviet Writers' Congress, Gorki formulates the methods of Socialist realism which becomes the official artistic doctrine to aid the class struggle and the building of a Socialist State. M Matiushin dies.

1935 The first stretch of the Moscow Underground is opened (the second was opened in 1938). The Federal Association of Inventors and Masters of Soviet Photographic Art hold exhibitions in Moscow with the participation of Rodchenko. K Malevich dies. El Lissitsky's album for the Fifteen Year Jublilee of the Red Army is published. Continuation of the purges in State and Party leadership which began in December 1934, after the murder of Kirov, the Leningrad Party Chief.

1936–1940	Forced collectivisation is completed, official announcement of the triumph of Socialism which had roots in the new constitution accepted by the 8th Soviet Congress (the Stalin Constitution). First show trial of politicians accused of treason (Sinoviev, Karmeniev and others), second show trial 1937, third trial 1938 (Bucharin). Commencement of the Third Five Year Plan (1938–42). Final rejection of formal experiments in architecture, visual art and performing art; dislike of Western cosmopolitan Modernism, stronger propagation of Socialist Realism. 1937 B Jofan makes designs for a restructuring of the Moscow city centre; World Exhibition in Paris with a Soviet Pavilion. 1938, a gallery for industrial art and interior design is created at the Architectural Academy. G Klutsis is arrested and deported. 1939 Farming Exhibition in Moscow with pavilions for the republics of the Union; World Exhibition in New York, N Suetin and K Roshdestvensky design the Soviet Pavilion.
1941–1945	Nazi Germany invades the Soviet Union, World War II. Art helps to fight Fascism – in the army studio M Grekov, poster production increases. 1941 El Lissitsky dies. 1944 Kandinsky dies. 1945 the Central Art Schools are reopened in Moscow (B Stroganov) and Leningrad (W I Muchina).
1946–1953	Commencement of the Fourth Five Year Plan (1946–50). 1946 governmental reforms, the Ministerial Council replaces the Council of People's Commissioners. An art and architectural association is created at the People's Commission for Machinery and Transport, first official design office. Greater opposition to cosmopolitanism and objectivism. Rebuilding of destroyed cities after general urban design plans. 1947–53, skyscrapers are erected in Moscow and the Lomonosov University is built (Lev Rudnev and others). 1946 M Ginsburg dies. 1948 D Shterenberg dies. 1949 A Exter dies. 1953 Tatlin dies. 1949 Council for Economic Cooperation with other Socialist

countries is founded. 1952 Moscow underground is enlarged (Komsomskaia Station and others). 1953 Stalin dies, N Krushchev becomes First Secretary of the Central Committee of the Communist Party. A new direction in foreign and local affairs is taken.

1954–1964	1954 N Suetin dies. 1955 Congress of Soviet Architects, decrees for new directions in urban planning and mass housing projects. 1956 commencement of the Sixth Five Year Plan, abandoned in 1959. 20th Party Congress with Khrushchev's secret speech about Stalin's reign of terror, rejection of the personality cult. Rodchenko dies. Rejection of the rigidity of Socialist Realism in art. 1957 World Festival of Youth and Students in Moscow. 1958, USSR takes part in the World Exhibition in Moscow. V Stepanova dies. 1958 commencement of the Seventh Five Year Plan. Exhibition of Soviet Feats (WDNCH) opens in Moscow, R Kliks is the leading designer. 1960, completion of the Tran-Siberian Railway. 1962, general discussions about the possibility of economic reform with decentralisation of companies. Decree of the Ministerial Council to improve machinery. Research Institute for Technological Aesthetics is created (VNIITE). Group for Kinetic Art (Dvishenie) is created in Moscow. 1964, first edition of the *Technological Aesthetics* periodical. Khrushchev is deposed, L Brezhnev becomes First Secretary of the Party, A Kossygin becomes President.
1965–1975	1965 The Scientific Research Institute for Technological Aesthetics (VNIITE) becomes a member of the umbrella organisation of design councils ICSID. First Industrial Design Conference (federal). 1965 23rd Party Congress of the Communist Party, arguments about reforms brought about by Khrushchev. A unified State system for the organisation of industrial design is created: VNIITE branches in Leningrad, Kiev, Minsk and other cities. Two thematic exhibitions about design. 1967 the USSR partici-

pates in the World Exhibition in Montreal. The Industrial Aesthetics in the USA exhibition takes place in Moscow. The *Senesh* Seminar is transformed into the Central Teaching and Experimental Studio for Artistic Planning at the Design Council. 1968 the Council of Ministers decides on 'greater use of the achievements of technological aesthetics in the economy'. 1969 the Central Committee of the Communist Party makes propositions about oppositional elements in the Party and amongst the people. 1970 the USSR takes part at Expo 70 in Montreal with the leadership of K Roshdestvensky. Greater influence of the twenties in art (on the poster, for example). 1971 commencement of the Ninth Five Year Plan (1971–75). Departments of industrial design are created in factories, institutions and ministeries. 1972 Second Federal Conference of Industrial Designers. 1974 Raymond Loewy visits Moscow, 1975 Ninth International Conference of the Design Councils (ICSID). Federal competition for designing mass-produced furniture, the Mebar Project is presented. 1973–75 Conference for Security and Co-operation in Helsinki and Geneva.

1976–
1984

A new constitution replaces the Stalin Constitution of 1936, the power of the Party is consolidated. The Central Committee of the Communist Party and the Council of Ministers decide to develop production of consumer goods and to raise standards of quality. 'Standards for making reports on the quality of new consumer items' are set up by the State Committee for Science and Technology and by the Ministry of Trade. First exhibition of young designers in Moscow. 1977 the Centre for Technological Aesthetics and the exhibition *Technological Aesthetics Create Quality* are opened in Moscow, dedicated to the 60th Anniversary of the Soviet Power. 1978 founding of the Committee for Technological Aesthetics. Federal conference on *Objective Living Conditions and the Needs of Man.* Second exhibition of young designers (*Design*

and the City). 1980 Olympic Games in Moscow. The dissident A Sacharov is exiled. 1981 26th Party Conference, commencement of the Eleventh Five Year Plan. *High-Quality and Effective Design* exhibition shown at the federal show (VDNCH). 1982 Brezhnev dies, J Andropov is Secretary-General of the Communist Party until 1984, succeeded by K Tshernenko. 1984 *Autoprom 84* exhibition, marking sixty years of Soviet automobile industry. First VNIITE seminar on 'Experimental Design' (material, technology, structure). The Mayakovsky Museum in Moscow shows the exhibition *Mayakovsky and Production Art,* federal exhibition on design and artistic design.

1985–
1991

M Gorbachev succeeds Tshernenko as Secretary-General of the Communist Party. Federal exhibition (VDNCH) *Scientific Progress 85* in Moscow. Further VNIITE seminar on 'Experimental Design' (colour and light). 1986 27th Party Congress of the Communist Party, commencement of the Twelfth Five Year Plan, a programme of wide social and economic reform in the spirit of perestroika and glasnost is set up. VNIITE seminar on 'Experimental Design' (structure and form). 1987 new company law, more rights for factories and companies. Founding Congress of the Soviet Design Council, design councils are set up in the republics. VNIITE seminar on 'Experimental Design' (dynamic and kinematic forms in design). Federal exhibition *Masters of Culture for Peace* with participation of designers. Exhibition of avant-garde art and the social climate of the twenties (*New Art – New Ways Of Life)* in Moscow. 1988 further VNIITE seminar on 'Experimental Design' (visual culture – visual thinking) and opening of the *Designers=Artists Exhibition* in Moscow. First federal student design competition. 1989 founding of the Moscow branch of the Design Council of the USSR. VNIITE seminar on 'Experimental design' (design and fashion). Second federal student design competition. 1990 numerous exhibitions of Soviet designers at home and abroad eg Paris, Tokyo, Budapest, Frankfurt, Italy and Argentina. Third federal student design competition, Charkov. 1991 Soviet-American conference and exhibition in Moscow (*Graphicon 91*, computer graphics). *Design in Moscow Exhibition* in Berlin. The Russian Design Council is founded. B Yeltsin is elected President of Russia, Gorbachev steps down as Secretary-General of the Communist Party, also as President of the Soviet Union in December. Founding of the Community of Independent States (CIS).

1992–
1994

Conference to found a successor to the Design Council of the USSR. First meeting of the Russian Design Council, Novgorod. *Design As Art Exhibition* in Moscow, the International Design Centre (IDZ) in Berlin presents the councils of Moscow and St Petersburg, participation at the *Interstoff* in Frankfurt. 1993 *Design and Culture In The Twentieth Century Conference* in Moscow at the Russian Academy of Arts and at the Tretiakov Gallery. International competition for animation and computer graphics *Anigraf 93* in Moscow.

Bibliography – A Selection

175

Authors' names and other names are printed here as in the original transcripts.

Afanasjew, Kyrill N: *Ideen – Projekte – Bauten, Sowjetische Architektur 1917–1932,* Dresden, 1973.

Anikst, Michail (ed): *Soviet Commercial Design of the Twenties,* London, 1987.

Architecture de papier d'URSS, exhibition catalogue, Paris, 1988.

Art into Life, Russian Constructivism 1914–1932, exhibition catalogue, New York, 1990.

Baron, Stephanie and Tuchman, Maurice (eds): *The Avant-Garde in Russia 1910–1930,* exhibition catalogue, Cambridge, Massachussetts, 1980.

Borisowa, Elena and Sternin, Grigori J: *Jugendstil in Rußland, Architektur, Interieurs, bildende und angewandte Kunst,* Stuttgart, 1988.

Bowlt, John E (ed): *Russian Art of the Avant-Garde: Theory and Criticism 1922–1934, (New York 1976),* London, 1988.

Boym, Constantin: *New Russian design,* New York, 1992.

Chan-Magomedow, Selim O: *Pioniere der sowjetischen Architektur, Der Weg zur neuen sowjetischen Architektur in den zwanziger und zu Beginn der dreißiger Jahre,* Dresden, 1983.

Cook, Catherine (ed): *Russian Avant-Garde and Architecture,* New York, 1983.

Dabrowski, Magdalene (ed): *Ljubow Popowa, 1889–1924,* exhibition catalogue, Munich, 1991.

Elliot, David (ed): *Art into Production, Soviet Textiles, Fashion and Ceramics,* exhibition catalogue, Oxford, 1984.

Fitzpatrick, Sheila: *Cultural Revolution in Russia, 1928–1931,* Bloomington, Indiana, 1978.

Guerman, Michail (ed): *Art of the October Revolution,* New York, 1979

Khan-Magomedow, Selim O: *Rodchenko,*

The Complete Work, edited by Vieri Quilici, Cambridge, Massachussetts, 1987.

Khan-Magomedow, Selim O: *VCHUTEMAS Moscou 1920–1930,* Paris, 1990.

Klotz, Heinrich, and Rappaport, Alexander: *Paper Architecture, New Projects from the Soviet Union,* New York, 1990.

Lobanov-Rostovsky, Nina: *Revolutionary Ceramics, Soviet Porcelain 1917–1927,* New York, 1990.

Lodder, Christina: *Russian Constructivism,* New Haven and London, 1983.

Nakov, Andrei B (ed): *El Lissitzky, 1889–1941, Retrospektive,* exhibition catalogue, Frankfurt am Main and Berlin, 1988.

Noever, Peter (ed): *Alexander M. Rodtschenko, Warwara Stepanowa, Die Zukunft ist unser einziges Ziel...,* (Our Only Aim is the Future), exhibition catalogue, Munich, 1991.

Russische Architektuur en Stedebouw 1917–1933, exhibition catalogue, Eindhoven, 1969.

Russische und Sowjetische Kunst 1910–1932, exhibition catalogue, Vienna, 1988.

Schadowa, Larissa A: *Malewitsch, Kasimir Malewitsch und sein Kreis,* Munich, 1982.

Shadowa, Larissa Alexejevna (ed): *Tatlin,* London, 1988.

Strizhenova, Tatiana: *Soviet Costume and Textiles 1917–1945,* Moscow, Paris and Verona, 1991.

Tolstoi, Vladimir; Bibikova, Irina, and Cook, Catherine: *Street Art of the Revolution, Festivals and Celebrations in Russia 1918–1933,* London, 1990.

Von der Malerei zum Design, Russische konstruktivistische Kunst der zwanziger Jahre, exhibition catalogue, Cologne, 1981.

Wladimir Tatlin 1885–1953, exhibition catalogue, (German–Russian), Cologne, 1993.

Wolter, Bettina-Martine, and Schwenk, Bernhart (eds): *Die große Utopie, Die russische Avantgarde 1915–1932,* exhibition catalogue, Frankfurt am Main, 1992.

Names Index